# THE
# INDECISIVENESS OF MODERN WAR

# THE INDECISIVENESS
# OF MODERN WAR

## AND OTHER ESSAYS

BY

## J. HOLLAND ROSE, Litt.D.

FELLOW OF CHRIST'S COLLEGE, CAMBRIDGE ; VERE HARMSWORTH PROFESSOR OF NAVAL
HISTORY, UNIVERSITY OF CAMBRIDGE ; HON. LITT.D., UNIVERSITY OF MANCHESTER ;
HON. LL.D., UNIVERSITY OF NEBRASKA AND OF AMHERST COLLEGE, MASS.

KENNIKAT PRESS, INC./PORT WASHINGTON, N. Y.

THE INDECISIVENESS OF MODERN WAR

First Published in 1927
Reissued in 1968 by Kennikat Press
Library of Congress Catalog Card No: 68-15834
Manufactured in the United States of America

# PREFACE

THESE essays are the outcome of many years of study of
the problems of war and national policy. The first two
set forth the conclusions to which, I believe, every open-
minded student must come if he contrasts the prolonged
deadlock in the North Sea and on the Western Front in
1914–18 with what was achieved by the weak, slow fleets
and small professional armies of earlier times. This strange
contrast has long impressed me ; and, at the risk of seeming
to exaggerate its import, I have felt impelled to point it
out. History would abdicate one of her functions if she did
not examine the causes of the mass-wastage into which
mass-warfare has degenerated. It is also demonstrable that
the study of Admiral Duckworth's expedition to Constantinople in 1807 should have saved England from the glorious
but disastrous venture of 1915. His final decision, which
I have quoted (pp. 177, 179), stated emphatically the condition on which alone success could reasonably be expected ;
and the advent of the mine, torpedo and machine-gun ought
to have added point to his warning. Why was not that
warning taken into account at Whitehall early in 1915 ?

The other essays deal with subjects bearing on national
safety and expansion, the balance of power in the Mediterranean, the ultimate dependence of India on Sea Power,
certain aspects of the careers of Napoleon and Nelson, the
well-being of the fleet in 1805, our acquisition of Malta,
and, finally, the comparatively recent growth of the spirit

of comradeship at sea. For permission to re-publish Nos. V., VI., VIII. and XI., I am indebted to the editorial committees of *The Indian Historical Journal, The Cambridge Historical Journal, The Mariner's Mirror*, and the Royal Society of Literature. On the topics treated in Essay I. I have received valuable advice from Admiral Sir William Henderson ; and on those of Essay II. from Lieut.-Colonel F. Moloney, R.E., and Major G. K. Rose, M.C. Other friends have read and criticised the remaining essays. One and all I thank them ; but mine alone is the responsibility for the opinions finally expressed.

J. H. R.

CAMBRIDGE, *January* 12, 1927.

# CONTENTS

# THE
# INDECISIVENESS OF MODERN WAR

# I

## THE INDECISIVENESS OF MODERN NAVAL WAR[1]

I should say the majority of our naval *personnel* entered upon the Great War with a sort of general impression, with no historical backing, that a war at sea opened with a decisive battle in which both sides fought to a finish.—" The Times," March 4, 1926.

THE term " indecisive " as applied to modern warfare is, of course, relative. I use it here to indicate the comparatively slight result that was achieved by the naval and military operations in the last war, when we measure that result against the enormous mass of the forces set in motion and the losses in life and treasure sustained by the chief combatants. Omitting all reference to the financial waste of the World War, which is incalculable, we may note the tale of sacrifice in lives ; for that is now known with something like accuracy, except in regard to Japan and Turkey. It appears that the other belligerent nations (inclusive of the U.S.) lost nearly $8\frac{1}{2}$ million sailors and soldiers killed dead or of illness. So far as is known, this total exceeds any that is recorded in history. Perhaps it is nearly equalled in proportion to population by the losses sustained in the Thirty Years War ; but those losses are conjectural, and were due largely to disease and famine among the civilian population, whereas, owing to the growth of medical science and the spread of philanthropic agencies, the number of deaths of that description among civilians and soldiers in wartime is now far smaller than in the Thirty Years War. Certain it is that the number of nearly

[1] Read to the Royal Institution, London, on March 18, 1926.

$8\frac{1}{2}$ million casualties in $4\frac{1}{4}$ years far exceeds the wastage ever before recorded among combatants.

If, on the other hand, we measure this appalling total against the results actually achieved by direct naval and military operations, the contrast is startling. Experts at the Staff Colleges are investigating this phenomenon, and are trying to account for it on technical grounds. In this paper I shall avoid technical questions, so far as possible, and try to throw the light of history upon the problem. But the inquiry will lead us inevitably to the question whether recent scientific and mechanical inventions have not largely contributed to the present singular situation.

Indecisiveness is, of course, no new feature in battles at sea. It characterised earlier periods, especially that from 1690 to 1779, which was dominated by the tactic of line acting against line. This formation was the outcome of the great development of gun-power in a broadside ; for it enabled all the ships' broadsides, without blanking each other, to bear on the enemy. Therefore it marked an advance on the earlier custom (perhaps reminiscent of the galley age) of a series of groups charging the enemy, generally with very confused results. But when, early in the eighteenth century, the line tactic was pushed to a pedantic extreme, it proved to be fatal to all initiative, the outcome being those typical battles of slow attrition and meagre results, Beachy Head (1690), Malaga (1704) and Toulon (1744). Rodney, Duncan, and Nelson successively modified or even broke up the long unwieldy line with the view of effecting a concentration on part of the hostile array ; and their efforts (curiously parallel to those of Frederic and Napoleon on land) led to brilliant victories. Nelson's famous memorandum of October 9, 1805 testifies to his anxiety to discover a method of approach less slow and cumbrous than that of the line ; and though in practice he modified that plan at Trafalgar, yet his supreme tactical effort on October 21 (his nautical will and testament) seemed to challenge his countrymen to further developments in this direction.

It was not to be. The introduction of steam-power of course facilitated the formation of a line of battle and perhaps furnished the reason why that tactic became stereotyped. On the other hand the armouring of ships, the contest between the gun and armour, and consequent enormous growth of tonnage increased the length of the line of a modern fleet. The result is that no fleet normally cruises in that formation ; and if an enemy approaches, the problem of quickly forming line ahead for battle becomes one of vital importance, on which the fate of nations may turn.

Consider the case of the Russian fleet before the Battle of Tsushima on May 27, 1905. In more ways than one it bears on our inquiry ; for it shows that a meeting between two hostile fleets of approximately equal strength may lead to the utter overthrow of the one which on paper appears to have a slight advantage in gun-power. Rojdestvensky's fleet, which left Cronstadt in two sections, comprised five first-class, three second-class, and three third-class battleships, in all mounting 41 heavy guns ; while his opponent, Admiral Togo, marshalled only four first-class battleships, none of the second and third classes, but eight very efficient armoured cruisers as against one Russian. The Japanese fleet, therefore, carried only 17 heavy guns, but had a great superiority in 8-inch and 6-inch weapons, viz. 110 to 49. It also steamed 15 or 16 knots to the enemy's 10 or 11 ; [1] and the Japanese crews far excelled the Russians in skill, gunnery, and *moral*. The evidence presented in that pathetic book " Rasplata " (" The Reckoning ") proves that the Russian officers knew that they were sent out to certain defeat. As they neared Japan one of them, pointing to their course on the chart, exclaimed "Via dolorosa";[2] the captain of the " Ural " wanted to disarm her ; [3] and all of them cursed the over-confident bureaucrats of Petersburg who sent them out to what seamen knew to be

---

[1] H. W. Wilson, " Battleships in Action " (1926), vol. i. p. 244.
[2] Semenoff, " Rasplata," p. 471.
[3] Politovsky, " From Libau to Tsushima," p. 297.

disaster. Then, too, on the day of battle, Togo, already in single line, came upon them while still formed in two nearly parallel columns, which hindered each other's fire [1] In vain did Rojdestvensky seek betimes to form a single line ahead. Togo caught him while in the midst of that manœuvre, and the deadly fire of the Japanese on the two leading ships partly disabled them and confused the whole Russian fleet. Victory soon inclined to the more disciplined fleet; but the victory was crushing because Togo caught the Russians in the act of forming line. Tsushima, then, was wholly exceptional, not a battle but a battue.

The Japanese victory at Tsushima was hailed as decisive proof of the superiority of the great gun. In reality it proved only the superiority of quick and accurate gunnery. The rapid succession of hits scored by the lighter Japanese artillery bewildered the Russian crews, one of the officers of the " Suvaroff " declaring : " I had never even imagined anything like it. Shells seemed to be pouring upon us incessantly." The meaning of it all was clearly discerned at Berlin and Wilhelmshafen. But in the nine years' interval before the Great War occurred notable developments in the long duel between gun and armour. The incoming of the 13·5-inch and 15-inch gun necessitated a further strengthening of armour and an increase in the size of the battleship, as was seen successively in the " King George " class and the " Queen Elizabeths." But the same years also witnessed the development of high explosives and the enhanced efficiency of torpedoes and mines. Further, by the year 1914 aircraft and wireless telegraphy were so far advanced as greatly to complicate the already complex problems of naval warfare. None of these later inventions had counted for much at Tsushima. Aircraft and wireless telegraphy were then in their infancy ; and the roughness of the sea almost paralysed the action of torpedo craft. The gun there held undisputed sway.

But it was not so at Jutland on May 31, 1916. In the interval of eleven years the conditions of naval warfare had

[1] Barfleur, " Naval Policy," ch. vii., esp. pp. 169, 171, 175.

greatly changed. Wireless telegraphy had put the commander-in-chief more and more closely in touch with the Admiralty, which body now frequently transmitted news as to the enemy's movements, and to some extent (as yet unknown) controlled those of its executant. On the other hand the anxieties of the commander were immeasurably increased by hostile aircraft and still more by the unseen peril of the submarine and mine.

We may pause here to note the wider significance of these inventions. Unquestionably they have tended to revolutionise naval warfare. Indeed, it is not too much to say that by the year 1914 scientific discoveries had outpaced the ability of man either to gauge their efficacy or to work them all with full confidence. Man has become more and more the victim of the mechanism which he has created. He is in the grip of his own mechanical monster, for his powers have not developed *pari passu*. Rather have they been dwarfed by the feeling of his own impotence. Also commanders-in-chief are apt to be oppressed by a sense of overwhelming responsibility when wielding the vast and complex mechanism of modern war ; and to this fundamental cause may be ascribed the reason why campaigns, in proportion to the masses employed, have become singularly barren of decisive results.

For there is this further consideration. Nations do not normally go to war unless their own strength or the aid of allies gives them approximately an equality of force with the enemy. The outcome of this prudent diplomacy is that great national struggles tend to occur only between approximately equal masses ; and the solidity of the modern national State generally furnishes the means of persevering with a wasteful fury unknown in former ages of small States and mere popguns. Nowadays vast stores of men and money are available, and all the resources of science are pressed into the service, the result being a war-complex puzzling even to the experts on this or that section of it, and utterly baffling to the civilian Ministers who affect to ride the hurricane and direct the storm.

Here we approach the problem of "the politicians." Avoiding the rhetoric which this subject always evokes from experts, we must still admit that the progress of events, which has increased the means of destruction, has also weakened the political organism which directs them. Demos is now enthroned ; but the democratic enthusiasm which embattled the first citizen armies has, since the days of Napoleon I., given us citizen·committees to control them. Now democracy tends to bring to the front the ablest debaters rather than the most capable administrators, and the latter, along with the naval and military experts, who, when once the guns have spoken, ought to have the last word, are generally subordinated to the men who can manage Parliament.[1]  To provide masses of men and money is now the chief task of a War Cabinet ; and these it furnishes to a degree never known before.  But it also controls war policy and war measures, with the result that the forces soon marshalled dwarf those of the Napoleonic era, but are wielded in a way less Napoleonic than bureaucratic.  To this fundamental cause we may assign the empirical efforts which characterised the last war.  They often resulted from compromises arrived at in the War Cabinet.  Many of the war puzzles probably have their explanation in the large share of control necessarily assigned to civilians who are thrust into impossible positions.  In short, the modern democratic-national State is not well adapted to the working of the complicated war-machine of to-day.

Further, the commander-in-chief of a great fleet now confronts responsibilities dwarfing those of the age of Nelson.  The stream of wireless messages from Whitehall and from his own scouts (naval, aerial, and submarine) implies an untiring brain, always receptive, always judicial. Yet the recipient must be always fresh for every new emergency.  Moreover, the commander cannot fail to be oppressed by the enormous mass and costliness of his fleet,

---

[1] This does not apply so much to the Central Empires.  But even at Berlin and Vienna public opinion counted for more than was suspected in 1914–18.

embodying as it does the skill and resources of a great nation ; and he now has to face not merely visible dangers but also the invisible dangers aforesaid. Whether the menace from hostile submarines and aircraft was not over-rated in the last war is a question that is now hotly discussed. But it cannot be doubted that naval strategy was profoundly affected by the recent developments of those arms, which occurred at the time when the advent of the " super-Dreadnought " offered a more costly and tempting objective.

Lord Fisher, the father of the " Dreadnought," was (contrary to popular belief) the inculcator of a cautious strategy ; and caution is writ large over the naval history of 1914–16. The smashing blows which were generally expected did not fall. On the contrary, both sides played a waiting game which surprised all except a few experts. In signal contrast to the presumption of the Russian Government in 1904–5 was the circumspection of the British and German Admiralties in 1914–16. Far from sending a battle-fleet over a great extent of sea to fight a battle in the enemy's waters, as the Tsar's advisers had done, the British and Germans each sought to tempt the other to come across the North Sea and fight near the hostile coasts. Capitan Gros states that the Germans fully expected our fleet to attack theirs in or near Wilhelmshafen, and their whole plan was upset by the unexpected caution of Admiral Jellicoe.[1]

The reasons underlying this policy of tempting the enemy out into your own waters are these :

(1) If he comes right across the North Sea, his approach will probably be detected by the many scouts on the watch for him, and he may be seriously damaged in a minefield or by submarines before coming to close quarters.

(2) Great fleets must now be guarded by destroyers and submarines, which cannot operate far from their base. It

[1] O. Gros, " Der Krieg zur Nordsee," p. 5. This admission supplies ample justification for British caution.

is doubtful whether a great battle can be fought very far from the hostile bases.[1]

(3) After a battle fought near the enemy's coasts, the injured ships will find great difficulty in making their way back across the North Sea, when hostile aircraft and submarines are waiting to finish them off. (After June 1, 1916, the " Marlborough " had some difficulty in getting away into the Humber, and the " Warspite " into Rosyth ; also the " Warrior " had to be abandoned.)

Further (to take a broader strategic view) it was correct strategy for the Germans to maintain a vigilant defensive. Their High Sea Fleet was weaker than Admiral Jellicoe's Grand Fleet. Therefore of set purpose the Germans held back their fleet in the strongly fortified harbours of Wilhelmshafen and Kiel, with the intention of offering battle when they had succeeded in wearing down the British navy by submarines and mines. Of course they made sorties for exercise and remained always ready to strike at Admiral Jellicoe if he gave them a chance. Such a chance would come if he attacked the powerful batteries of Heligoland or Wilhelmshafen, as the Germans fully expected him to do. But he was far too wise to take so false a step. Based on the natural harbour, Scapa Flow, he dominated the northern exit of the North Sea. As Capitan Gros says : " England blockades us already by her geographical position." [2] Jellicoe did but emphasise and clinch our natural strategic advantage. Thus began that long blockade of Germany which finally became almost unendurable to her. Parts of the Grand Fleet took periodical sweeps into the North Sea, in the hope of tempting the enemy out, but the Germans were not to be tempted out for a fight before "the day."

---

[1] At present it seems likely that a struggle between the American and Japanese battle-fleets for the control of the Pacific would present insoluble problems. It might become farcical.

[2] Gros, p. 43. Mr. Winston Churchill argues (" World Crisis," i. p. 244) that the German fleet should have been attacked soon because our preponderance by new construction would increase. But in his notes of August 8 and October 8 he commends their trust in " equalising " tactics and their defensive strategy.

There was another lure which might have brought them out from Wilhelmshafen in mid-August 1914, viz., the endless procession of troop-ships and store-ships conveying the British Expeditionary Force to France. That valuable prize was then crossing the Channel, chiefly from Southampton to Le Havre ; and it was guarded ostensibly by the second-line battleships of the Allies, left behind in the Channel ports. These were inferior in strength to the German High Sea Fleet. But in reality the chief protec-tion to our transports was the Grand Fleet at Scapa Flow. Admiral Jellicoe, when warned (as he would at once be by wireless) that the German warships were making for the English Channel, could have caught them during their retirement to Wilhelmshafen. The German High Command recognised this fact. It was probable that their High Sea Fleet would sink some British transports in mid-Channel ; but it was still more probable that, thanks to the invisible but potent agency of wireless telegraphy, that fleet would end up with disaster. After using up much of their fuel (for the German ships and destroyers were built with a view to a battle near their own base) they would be caught at a disadvantage before returning to port. Accordingly, they never made the attempt.[1] Indeed Admiral Scheer himself has stated that to do so would have been a false move, and that the right way of neutralising the British army in France and Flanders was by the German army driving it back to the French coast.[2]

This admission is highly significant. It implies that the Germans preferred to fight the two desperate series of battles round Ypres for that purpose, rather than to attempt to destroy or cripple the British army while it was crossing the Channel. In other words, they preferred what they considered safe military action to endangering their main

[1] The brilliant British success near Heligoland on August 28, 1914 was primarily due to the initiative of our Admiralty ; and the German counterstroke which led to the Battle of the Dogger Bank (January 24, 1915), was only part of their wearing-down game.

[2] Scheer, " The High Sea Fleet," p. 63.

battle-fleet while Admiral Jellicoe was ready to attack it. Therefore the German navy was not used for an object which, if attained, might have dealt the Allied armies a deadly blow. Its inactivity, in face of this great opportunity, was a severe disappointment to the German people ; but in a strategic sense it was the correct course not to hazard the High Sea Fleet unduly while Jellicoe's great force was intact. We may note again that the caution of the German Admiralty rested on the assumption that, owing to wireless telegraphy, a surprise attack on the British transports would entail swift and terrible punishment.[1] The change in modern warfare produced by wireless here received telling illustration. It is a change of far-reaching import ;[2] for though the transmission of news by wireless has not seldom been interrupted by the enemy (" jammed " is the slang term) yet in the main it operated successfully ; and there can be little doubt that it has revolutionised naval warfare.[3] In the olden times an admiral never knew what was going on beyond the horizon. Now he is in communication with the Admiralty at London, which, in its turn, is receiving frequent messages from scouts as to the enemy's moves. Therefore in normal weather conditions the element of surprise, which has been the chief factor in the achievement of the great naval victories, has been almost eliminated : and the time of watching the enemy for an opportunity which never comes may be indefinitely prolonged.

These remarks apply chiefly to the battle-fleets. For cruisers, destroyers, and submarines there will always be

[1] Gros, p. 83. So, too, W. Churchill (i. pp. 257-259). After the German losses at the Battle of Heligoland (August 28), the Kaiser disallowed sorties "unless approved by His Majesty in advance" (Tirpitz, "Mems." p. 357). So, too, again in mid-December.

[2] In 1905 wireless worked very badly on the Russian fleet. (See Semenoff, p. 458.)

[3] One of its weaknesses is that wireless stations can be easily destroyed. The British Pacific squadron destroyed all the five German stations in the Pacific within two months (W. Churchill, i. 295). Another is that by means of directional stations the position of an enemy ship which uses its wireless installation can be traced (ibid. p. 463).

plenty of surprises : but contact between great fleets will probably be more and more difficult to attain. If we may judge by the events of 1914–16, the commander of the weaker fleet will try to tempt the enemy as far as possible away from his own base and into a trap ; while the enemy will be equally determined not to be decoyed and trapped. On August 14, 1914 the German Commander-in-Chief, Ingenohl, warned his men that that was the correct German policy. The most important parts of his Order of the Day are as follows :

" The enemy intends to compel us to come with our battleships to his coasts and there to fall a victim to his mines and submarines. *We are not going to oblige the enemy thus. But they must and will come to us some day.* And then will be *the day of reckoning.* The moment the enemy comes within our range, he shall find us waiting for him. *It is therefore our duty not to lose patience, but to hold ourselves ready at all times to profit by the favourable moment.*" [1]

These statements explain why, for the main fleets, the last naval war was pre-eminently a war of waiting. The period of watching lasted twenty-two months. The wearing-down game was played by both sides with great skill— on our side by periodic and extensive sweeps in the North Sea (highly serviceable as maintaining the *moral* and efficiency of the British crews) ; on the German side by occasional restricted sorties, but more often by submarine action and minelaying. Herein they attained a certain measure of success. So active were their submarines (though at first comparatively small and of limited range) as for a time to induce Admiral Jellicoe with the bulk of the Grand Fleet to leave Scapa Flow (where no booms or other defences had been prepared before the war) and to take refuge in Lough Swilly (Oct.-Nov. 1914).[2] This

---

[1] Scheer, "High Sea Fleet," p. 40. So too O. Gros, "Der Krieg zur Nordsee" (1920), p. 58. See H. W. Wilson, vol. ii. pp. 9, 15, 81 for criticisms on German timidity in 1914.

[2] Corbett, i. 239-40. Mr. Winston Churchill (i. p. 381) claims that natural difficulties at Scapa Flow precluded all likelihood of a hostile submarine entering.

singular occurrence is referred to by Admiral Jellicoe only in very brief and guarded terms, but in the following words we can discern the danger which threatened the Grand Fleet at Scapa Flow. After 23rd of October, when Lough Swilly was guarded by a boom, etc., he writes : " For the first time since the declaration of war the Fleet occupied a secure base." [1] This phrase *donne sérieusement à penser* ; for it implies that during many days the German submarine menace led to the withdrawal of the Grand Fleet to the north of Ireland and therefore to a temporary relaxation of the blockade of Germany. Even off Lough Swilly it suffered a severe loss : for on October 27, during a sweep outside, the " Audacious," third in the line, struck a mine laid by a German minelayer and sank. As the war progressed, the German submarines increased notably in power and zone of operation, with a corresponding increase of danger to the Grand Fleet, unless fully guarded by light cruisers, submarines, and aircraft.

Nevertheless, owing to the unceasing vigilance of Admiral Jellicoe and his splendid *personnel*, the Grand Fleet was not worn down to the extent hoped for by the Germans. On December 16, when the German fleet made its first important sortie, it numbered 13 Dreadnought battleships and 4 battle-cruisers against Jellicoe's 27 units.[2] Finally Admiral Scheer, the commander-in-chief who succeeded Ingenohl and von Pohl, sought to end the long and now unendurable blockade by bolder tactics. He himself rather boastfully phrased it thus in his official report : " England's purpose of strangling Germany economically, without seriously exposing her own fleet to the German guns, had to be defeated." [3] A more probable cause of his sortie may be found in the well-known fact that the fleet which long pursues a tame defensive, and does not have frequent exer-

---

[1] Jellicoe, "The Grand Fleet, 1914–1916," p. 147. So, too, Vice-Admiral Sir D. Beatty wrote on October 17, 1914 from Mull, "We are gradually being pushed out of the North Sea " (W. Churchill, i. 389).

[2] W. Churchill, i. p. 448, but see H. W. Wilson, ii. 9.

[3] Scheer, p. 176.

cises, suffers a distinct loss of *moral*. Scheer hoped to
entrap part of our fleet in a mine area ; but whether he
wanted anything more than that is considered by our
authorities to be very doubtful.

However, let us take his own account of his motives for
a sortie at its face value. He states that he had prepared
a plan for entrapping the British Grand Fleet. In brief it
was this. His High Sea Fleet, together with its cruisers
and destroyers, was to proceed from Wilhelmshafen secretly
northwards, while several units were to bombard heavily
the port of Sunderland. Scheer expected that the first and
second Battle Cruiser Squadrons, under Vice-Admiral Beatty,
which had by now been removed from Scapa to Rosyth,
would hasten out from the Firth of Forth so as to save
Sunderland ; and he had ordered a minefield to be sown
thickly in their probable track. Thereupon the German
fleet would be near at hand to finish off the survivors.
That is, he expected to deal only with the southern and
lighter portion of the Grand Fleet.

Here was a promising plan. It differed radically from
the sorties often attempted by our enemies in earlier wars.
For the most part those sorties were made with political
aims in view, generally the invasion of England or some
important possession. To such causes we owe the campaigns leading up to the battles of Barfleur, La Hogue,
Lagos, Quiberon, the Saints (1782), St. Vincent, and Camperdown. These campaigns and the resulting battles were
due to the enemy's prosecution of some important political
object. In other words, the enemy did not aim primarily
at the destruction of the British fleet, but rather at its
evasion.

At the end of May 1916, everything seemed to favour
Scheer's project. Why did it not succeed ? Because, by
a singular coincidence, it so happened that at that time
Admiral Jellicoe came out, probably with some hope of
meeting Scheer. But, so far as we know at present, the
meeting of the two fleets was fortuitous. Scheer chose
the date May 31 for his sortie because after that day it

would become necessary to call in the German submarines
which he had sent out some time previously to patrol the
line that the British would take from Scapa and Rosyth.
But there was a second reason, viz. that by May 31 important repairs to the powerful battle-cruiser " Seydlitz,"
would be completed ; and (as he states) " I had no intention of doing without that battle-cruiser." [1] The punc-
tuality of German dockyard work, therefore, fixed the date
of his sortie at May 31 ; and he came out, quite unconscious
of the fact that Jellicoe and Beatty were coming out. The
British Admiralty (so it seems from our present state of
knowledge) had not fully fathomed Scheer's plan, which he
of course kept secret. But it knew that certain units of
the German High Sea Fleet were putting out from Wilhelmshafen and mustering in the Jade Roads. Accordingly
it warned Jellicoe at Scapa Flow and Beatty at Rosyth,
with the result that they were on the *qui vive*. Owing to
Scheer's special precautions, the British Admiralty could
not ascertain when he set out ; [2] but suspicions were aroused
that some important move might be expected ; and it
seems that the Admiralty ordered the Grand Fleet to patrol
southwards. Admiral Jellicoe, in the very guarded narrative which he thought it prudent to publish in 1919,
states that he took the Grand Fleet to sea on May 30
merely for one of the periodical sweeps in the North Sea.
He desired to bring the German fleet to action, if the opportunity offered, but he was in doubt how far he might take
grave risks for his fleet in view of " the new conditions of
naval warfare." [3]

Seeing that the Germans only meant to fight if they could
catch a portion of our fleet at a disadvantage, it is clear
that the only great action of the war came about by chance.
And it was by a triple chance. We have seen that there
were two incidents which fixed the date of Scheer's sortie
for May 31. But a third chance supervened. It so hap-

[1] Scheer, p. 134.
[2] Corbett, iii. p. 326 ; Wilson, ii. 131.
[3] Jellicoe, " The Grand Fleet," p. 302.

pened that the British first Light Cruiser Squadron, under Commodore Sinclair, while feeling its way down the North Sea, sighted the smoke of a steamer, hull down in the east. Sinclair despatched the " Galatea " to see who she was ; and the " Galatea," while going after that harmless tramp, was sighted by a German destroyer, also sent to inquire what that vessel was. The German destroyer and her consorts made for the " Galatea's " smoke, and so steamed far enough west to sight Vice-Admiral Beatty's battle-cruisers some hours out from Rosyth, on their way to the rendezvous arranged with Admiral Jellicoe. Thus, owing to a third chance, May 31 was destined to see the meeting of the hostile battle-cruisers, which led on to that of the great battle fleets, but not until late in the afternoon of a somewhat misty day.[1] These exceptional occurrences determined the time and conditions of the battle. But for these three chances it is doubtful whether the main fleets would ever have met at all.

It is impossible here to discuss the details of the Battle of Jutland, the evidence on which is yet far from complete, besides being regrettably complicated by personal controversies. For our purpose we may note merely these outstanding facts :

(1) The British Grand Fleet, when united near the scene of conflict, numbered 28 battleships, all " Dreadnoughts " or "super-Dreadnoughts," as against 22 German battleships, of which 6 were pre-Dreadnought. Our battlecruisers numbered 9 to the German 5.

(2) Both the British and German battle-cruisers were so far ahead of their battle-fleets as to expose them to much danger if the enemy had known the actual situation.

(3) Neither Jellicoe nor Scheer knew it, because, owing to the misty conditions prevalent on that day, British and German aircraft could give little or no warning of the approach of the enemy. We had only one aeroplane scouting for the Grand Fleet ;[2] and the German scouting

---

[1] Scheer, pp. 141-152, admits that it was a chance meeting.
[2] " Jutland Despatches," 7 ; W. Churchill, i. 313.

airships did not go up on that day. If they had scouted successfully, the hostile fleets would never have met at all ; for Scheer did not want to fight the Grand Fleet.

(4) During the first phase of the battle (that between the battle-cruiser squadrons) Vice-Admiral Beatty, while heavily engaged, heard at 4.38 from the " Southampton " that the German battle-fleet was ahead. He therefore turned back northward so as to lure it towards the Grand Fleet.[1]

(5) News of the proximity of the German High Sea Fleet got through by wireless imperfectly to Admiral Jellicoe in the Grand Fleet about 4.50,[2] but not until 6.14 did he hear definitely from Vice-Admiral Beatty that that fleet was in sight to the S.S.W. Even then Jellicoe did not know its exact position. " Consequently, the deployment (of the Grand Fleet) was carried out under some disadvantage." [3]

(6) Into the controversy on this question it would be presumptuous for me to enter. But the late deployment of the Grand Fleet, from its cruising formation in parallel divisions into the battle formation of line ahead, is widely considered a leading cause why this superior force failed decisively to defeat the High Sea Fleet.

(7) Scheer had all along kept his 22 units in line ahead, and was therefore always ready for battle. He states that not until 6.25 P.M. (?) did he know that the Grand Fleet was ahead. Its deployment, begun at 6.15,[4] must then have been incomplete. There ensued a short but fierce engagement, which about 7.15 Scheer broke off by a " turn away " of his units all together, under cover of a charge made by his light craft against the Grand Fleet.[5]

(8) Twice during the pursuit Scheer repeated this manœuvre skilfully and successfully. The weather conditions favoured such tactics ; and for the most part the

---

[1] " Jutland Despatches," 10, 452.
[2] Beatty's flagship, " Lion," had its wireless shot away (Corbett, iii. 349).
[3] " Jutland Despatches," 16.
[4] *Ibid.* 458.
[5] Scheer's account in " The High Sea Fleet " is confused.

German gunners had the best of the light. Speaking generally, a scientific control of ships' fire from the flagship, " Iron Duke," was impossible. " Ships fired at what they could see while they could see it." [1]

(9) Thus, chance brought about the Battle of Jutland, and weather conditions largely accounted for its indecisiveness, the British 15-inch guns being very rarely able to make use of their long range to outclass the enemy.

(10) It seems probable that the conditions which may in the future bring about a decisive naval battle are either an act of administrative madness, such as sent the Russian fleet to disaster at Tsushima ; or the complete breakdown of the intelligence department of the weaker and slower fleet, so that it is thoroughly trapped ; or the resolve of both sides to fight to a finish on a long and clear day. How often are these conditions likely to occur ?

Further, a tactical success gained by the weaker side may avail little. At Jutland the Germans gained such a success ; for they lost one " pre-Dreadnought " and one battle-cruiser, and destroyed three British battle-cruisers and three armoured cruisers. Yet they did not break the British blockade of Germany, which Scheer declared to be his aim. As the Kaiser and he put forth a claim to a decisive victory, it was for them to clinch it by a second and greater and conscious effort. This they did not attempt. True, on August 18, 1916, Scheer came out as if for the resumption of his plan ; but one has only to read between the lines of his narrative to see that he was glad to get back without fighting.[2] Thereafter the High Sea Fleet made no important sortie.

In truth, the Battle of Jutland made no change whatever in the conduct of the naval war. The Grand Fleet resumed its blockade of Germany from Scapa as base, with occasional sweeps into the North Sea, while its rival remained almost entirely quiescent at Wilhelmshafen. The long watch, broken on May 31, June 1, and August 18,

---

[1] " Jutland Despatches," 12, 18.
[2] Scheer, ch. 11.

was now unbroken by any incident, and German commerce lay strangled. In fact, the situation now resembled that which came about after Trafalgar.[1] When Napoleon fully recognised his helplessness at sea, he recurred to warfare on British commerce. Such had been the policy of France after heavy naval defeats ; and her reliance on *la guerre de course* was a confession of naval inferiority. Similarly, not long after Jutland, the German Supreme War Council resolved to stake their all on commerce destruction—a device far more threatening to the overcrowded and industrial England of 1916 than it had been to the agricultural and sparsely peopled England of 1806.

Accordingly, in October 1916, the German Government ordered the resumption of submarine war against Allied commerce, a decision which involved the diversion of the submarines needed for service with Scheer's fleet to the task of commerce destruction. This step, Scheer avers, was disliked by the German navy ; and he himself disapproved of it as impairing the efficiency of his fleet. Certain it is that the prolonged inactivity of the German fleet (varied by only a few perfunctory sorties) brought about a serious decline in the *moral* of its crews. Dry-rot spread through the German navy with ever - increasing speed in 1918, until finally it produced the mutinies at Kiel and Wilhelmshafen. They in their turn started the German *débâcle* of November 1918. Thus the following out of the correct strategy of the weaker side involved ruin for that side. The Nemesis of prolonged inaction was Revolution.

To turn to our side of that wearisome game—had we any means of compelling the German fleet to come out and

---

[1] This is not to say that, strategically, Jutland equalled Trafalgar ; for Nelson practically destroyed the hostile fleet, while Jellicoe at most only " neutralised " it (if I may use Admiral Custance's term). But the results were not dissimilar. The so-called " command of the sea " has never been absolute. After Jutland the Germans expected to dispute it better by submarine action than by fleet action. But both before and after Jutland the Grand Fleet guarded our sea communications and clogged, or almost stopped, those of the enemy. Very rarely, if ever, can a superior fleet effect more than this.

fight ? None, surely, except the cumulative pressure of a long blockade on Germany's resources—a pressure which was doubled when the United States joined the Allies. That it was which finally decided the issue in 1918. Like the warfare on land, so, too, the maritime struggle was one of prolonged attrition, not so much on the German fleet as on German resources, *i.e.* in the last resort on the civilian population of Germany.

Was there any other way whereby British naval superiority could be effectively used ? It has recently been stated by an acknowledged authority that there was a better way—viz. by the destruction of the High Sea Fleet.[1] Granted. That alternative, if attainable, was certainly far more decisive than the policy of blockade from Scapa Flow, which he censures. But he does not point out how we were to destroy that fleet if it remained in a strongly fortified harbour. Was Admiral Jellicoe to assail Wilhelmshafen ? It is true that the First Lord of the Admiralty on one famous occasion urged that we must go and " dig them out." But that suggestion smacked less of strategy than of ratting. Indeed, there are very few, if any, means of forcing the enemy out of port by naval action if he is determined to play the waiting game, which, it is generally allowed, is his wisest course. He cannot now be blockaded closely ; for submarines and mines have made a close blockade impossible. Further, he cannot always be compelled to come out by threatening, or even by bombarding, coast towns. He will see through that game and act with caution, if at all.[2]

We must here notice an important difference between naval and military campaigns ; and I call attention to this difference because the ignoring of it has sometimes led to erroneous comparisons. True, naval and military campaigns can be compared in certain broad outlines ; but in one essential particular they differ fundamentally. It is

[1] Admiral Sir R. Custance, " A Study of War," p. 44.

[2] Jellicoe, " Grand Fleet," p. 459, states that the Grand Fleet could not act specially to prevent such bombardments.

this. There are rarely any key positions in the open sea. Important straits, *e.g.* those of Dover and of Gibraltar, are exceptional cases ; but for the most part the seas and the oceans are strategically one whole ; and no one area of open water is more valuable than another. If you command one area, you can, if fuel suffices, command all areas. In other words, the so-called command of the sea implies the ability to command the seas within striking distance.

But it is not so in land warfare. There topography counts for very much ; and the issue of a campaign may depend on the defence of an important city or a road centre. Even for the defence of a low hill, like Hill Sixty near Ypres, tens of thousands of men have laid down their lives. Thus it often happens that one general can compel another to fight in order to defend an important road centre, or it may be a pass, a river-crossing, or even a slight rise like that of Mont St. Jean. Friedland, Borodino, Leipzig, Quatre Bras, and Waterloo are five among many examples of such battles forced on the defenders. But no such compulsion can be exerted at sea ; for there are no key positions at sea (save in the case of straits or protected roadsteads), and the stronger fleet cannot compel the weaker fleet to come out and fight by such a tactical menace.[1] The only course now feasible is that of a comparatively distant blockade, and that, as it seems to me, is the wearisome and costly alternative to which naval warfare is likely to be reduced in the future, always provided that the weaker force plays a prudent game of waiting and watching.

Realising the futility of fleet action, the German Government, as we have seen, decided for unrestricted submarine action. I have no space in which to treat fully that phase of the war ; but the following remarks are apposite to our inquiry. First is the illuminating statement of the Austrian

---

[1] Some writers urged the seizure of Heligoland or Borcum in order to bring out the German fleet. But how were we to maintain a garrison there ? Such an effort would have provided an easy target for the German submarines based on the neighbouring estuaries. Lord Fisher's favourite plan of a great expedition to the Baltic is open to the same fatal objection, *i.e.* after German submarines became numerous and powerful.

Chancellor, Count Burian, that Germany staked everything on the success of a mechanical invention,[1] quite regardless of the moral and political issues which its application might raise. That invention, the submarine, was, however, extremely formidable. In fact, at no time in the history of war has an instrument of destruction attained a more deadly potency. Moreover, its victim, the merchantman, was apparently quite helpless. The bulk of the food brought to these islands comes in comparatively small cargo steamers in which speed and structural strength are sacrificed to carrying capacity. These steamers are slow and are easily sunk. Further, in order to prevent neutrals supplying us with the necessaries of life, the Germans resolved, after February 1, 1917, to treat Allied and neutral merchantmen alike. By this barbarous breach of the laws of war they inflicted terrible losses on neutrals. To take the case of one neutral, Norway : it is now known that the Norwegians lost during the war 1,239,283 tons of shipping ; also 1162 of their seamen were drowned, while about 1200 seamen disappeared, their fate being unknown.[2] A few of these losses, doubtless, were accidental, due to contact with mines ; but it is fair to assume that the great majority of these sinkings were intentional, the aim being at all costs to starve the British Isles into surrender by sinking even neutral merchantmen.

Now it may be admitted freely that this policy of ruthlessness at sea (*spurlos versenken*) came near to success in the spring of 1917. Nevertheless, after a year's trial, it failed. I can venture only on the following suggestions for its failure. The political rebound against these methods of frightfulness at sea was equally potent. It took the form of the declaration by the United States that Germany was in a state of war with them ; and other Powers declared against her for the same cause. The mechanical rebound was almost equally effective. The challenge to world-

---

[1] Burian, " Austria in Dissolution," p. 229.

[2] I am indebted to Professor W. Keilhau, of the University of Oslo, for these facts.

commerce met with a world-wide retort. Everywhere ship-building was pressed on with phenomenal rapidity, so that in the year 1918 the world's output of ships was nearly double what it had been in any previous year of peace. This fact is well worthy of notice. It proves that, when the world's need of shipping was the greatest, the total output of ships finally corresponded to that need, and restored the equilibrium which the ·Germans believed that they had upset to their own advantage.

Further, the merchantmen, when brought together in convoys and effectively guarded by light cruisers and destroyers, proved to be a means of attracting the submarines to their destruction. Naturally enough they made for the convoys in order to sink as many merchantmen as possible. But the light cruisers and destroyers kept a close watch and frequently sank the attacking submarines. Thus, though the merchantmen were generally helpless when caught singly, yet when under convoy they formed a capital lure, fatal to many a German submarine. One could not find a better example of what may be called the stabilising process of modern warfare. The collective intellect of man was equal to the emergency.

This fact is still more clearly demonstrated if we glance at the special anti-submarine inventions. The chief were the depth charge (which the Americans call the time-bomb), paravanes, hydrophones, and mine nets (i.e. netting with mines fixed to it). Thus many sciences were called upon to furnish contrivances for ridding the seas of those pests. A study of the submarine war is infinitely suggestive as revealing the wonderful resourcefulness of mankind when its interests are wounded at a vital point. At once all the universities, laboratories, and workshops of the world set to work to defeat the world's enemy ; and in all such cases, if the first sharp crisis can be tided over, the result will not be doubtful. That truth is one which cannot be too emphatically proclaimed and too widely recognised.

Consider again the variety of the means employed in anti-submarine warfare. They included aircraft, torpedo-boat destroyers, torpedo submarines, patrol vessels, swift motor boats, decoy ships, and armed merchantmen. All of these were effective in varying degrees. The following are, on good authority, believed to be the numbers of German submarines sunk by the different methods employed : depth charge, 35 ; mines, 34 ; torpedo submarines, 17 ; unknown methods, 17 ; blown up, 14 ; accident, 13 ; rammed by torpedo-boat destroyers and patrol vessels, 12 ; gunfire of the same, 12 ; miscellaneous methods (aircraft, paravanes, etc.) 12 ; decoy ships, 11; mine nets, 9 ; [1] rammed by men-of-war, 4 ; rammed by merchantmen, 4 ; total, 194. (Besides six, which were interned in neutral harbours).[2]

Admiral Jellicoe, writing in the spring of 1920, before the final figures were available, gives a total of 186 German submarines destroyed, viz., 5 in 1914, 19 in 1915, 25 in 1916, 66 in 1917, 71 in 1918. Taking even his figures, which are eight below the actual number, the increase in the rate of destruction of enemy submarines is very remarkable. It shows that the submarine challenge to the civilised world met with an increasingly effective retort ; and that even the use of this potent engine of destruction against the once helpless merchantman called into triumphant operation the law of reaction against the Power which made so unscrupulous a use of it.

Another set of figures is equally instructive. It shows the decline in the losses of British and foreign shipping due to German submarines. In the worst quarter of all, the spring of 1917, the losses totalled 2,236,934 tons. In the third quarter of 1918 they were only 915,513 tons. Moreover, as we have seen, the emergency in 1917 quickened enormously the world output of merchant shipping : so that in the third quarter of 1918 it amounted to 1,384,130

[1] Mine nets were laid down on several lines, notably the Dover Straits barrage, completed on February 8, 1917, and one farther west, not quite completed by November 1918 (A. Hurd, "The Merchant Navy," ii, 268-270): so too that between the Orkneys and Norway (see Sims, "The Victory at Sea," ch. 9).

[2] See W H. Wilson, ii. 231, for somewhat different estimates.

tons. Thus the output of shipping finally exceeded the losses by as much as 468,617 tons. Therefore the submarine campaign, which at first came dangerously near to success, was very far from accomplishing its purpose, even on the material side.[1] Further, the loss of about 5000 picked German sailors on the 194 submarines, nearly all of of which perished with all hands, dealt a deadly blow to the *personnel* of their navy, besides spreading deep discouragement among the crews ashore. Well, then, may the German naval writer Captain Persius arraign Tirpitz, the author of unrestricted submarine warfare, as the man who torpedoed Germany.[2]

Time will not admit of an adequate examination of another interesting development, that of the great gun and of fire-control. But I venture on these remarks. Undoubtedly the range and piercing power of the gun is a primary factor in success at sea. Indeed, from the time of Drake's dash into Cadiz in 1587, good guns and good gunnery have largely determined England's rise to naval supremacy. But in the development of every weapon there comes a time when the limits of efficiency are reached, especially when the limits of the nation's paying power are also reached. As has been suggested, the experience gained at the battle of Tsushima was not so much in favour of the great gun as of rapid and accurate firing from a larger number of medium-sized guns. The crews of the more heavily armed Russian battleships were from the start bewildered by the quick succession of hits, which thereafter silenced their guns and then disposed of the ships themselves. To win an initial and paralysing success now became the ideal in gunnery.

Already invention was proceeding towards fire-control from a fortified fighting-top, with the object of concentrating on the enemy the simultaneous fire of eight or ten heavy guns. In practice it was found impossible to work the fire-control with guns of different calibres. The 8-inch

---

[1] Jellicoe, " Crisis of the War," pp. 59-67, 224-227.
[2] Persius, " Der Seekrieg " (1919), p. 97.

or 9·2-inch gun was therefore done away with, and the new and improved 12-inch gun became the standard weapon. The outcome of the theory of concentrated fire was the " Dreadnought," carrying ten 12-inch guns and twenty-four small guns to repel light craft and submarines. Begun in 1905, and finished in 1906, she combined great offensive power with considerable defensive capacity and high speed. As she virtually superseded all former battleships, so too the new swift battle-cruiser, " Invincible," carrying eight 10-inch guns, rendered antiquated, or at least obsolescent, all the armoured cruisers.[1] The total effect was greatly to lessen the value of the large number of German ships constructed under the Kaiser's Navy Laws of 1898 and 1900.[2] Possibly the incoming of the " Dreadnought " may have deterred Germany from forcing on a rupture with the Triple Entente in the Balkan crisis of 1908–9 and the Agadir crisis of 1911 ; for, although supreme on land, she was then outclassed at sea. Moreover, the new battleships, which she constructed by way of retort, were too wide for her Kiel-North Sea Canal ; and until the canal was widened, as it was by June 1914, a war was inadvisable. Therefore the adoption of the " Dreadnought " class by Great Britain was possibly one cause for the postponement of the World War until after that date.

But in the ding-dong race between the gun and armour there is no finality. In 1911 came in the " King George V." class with ten 13·5-inch guns, which necessitated an increase in the displacement from 17,900 tons to 23,000 ; and in 1915 the " Queen Elizabeth," with ten 15-inch guns and a tonnage of 27,500. Neither is there finality in the naval competition between great and wealthy nations. If in 1905–09 we outpaced Germany by adopting the " Dreadnought," the latter spurted in and after 1908, so that, whereas at the end of the pre-Dreadnought period we had 27 battleships against her 18, yet by the year 1914 she had

[1] F. T. Jane, " The British Battle Fleet," ch. 14.
[2] For details see A. Hurd and H. Castle, " German Sea Power " (1913), ch. 5 and App.

26 Dreadnoughts or super-Dreadnoughts against our 39 ; that is, she finally recovered the proportion of 2 to 3 which she possessed in 1905–06.[1] Thus the naval rivalry of the two nations had merely carried the competition into vaster masses and higher figures ; but the relative position of the two navies remained virtually unchanged.

In one respect British naval construction suffered ; for the methodical Germans, who followed our lead, saw where improvements could be adopted with advantage ; and they devised Dreadnoughts of a range of action limited to the North Sea or Baltic, and with more inner protective armour and more water-tight compartments. British constructors, having to provide battleships of far wider range of action, were in this respect at a disadvantage. For a battleship is a compromise. The designer must try to satisfy the demands for seaworthiness, gun-power, defensive capacity, speed, wide range of action, and habitability. The Germans sacrificed the two last. I have been assured by naval officers who examined the German battleships after the surrender that they would rather run risks in British ships than be cooped up in the German hulls during a long voyage.

It is, then, clear that the advent of the super-Dreadnought has added to the difficulty of defending the British Empire. For such defence large numbers of effective, seaworthy, fast, well protected, and yet habitable units, having a wide range of action, are eminently desirable. A navy of this description of capital ship was possible twenty-five years ago when the " Majestic " class, costing about £1,000,000 each, formed the " line." A navy of " Queen Elizabeths " or " Hoods " is an impossibility. Therefore, from a review of the past, we must conclude that it is a mistake for the leading sea power to start vast and costly innovations in ship construction. While it is foolish to neglect obvious improvements, it is suicidal to initiate a competition in bulk, which implies a wholesale rebuilding of ships, plant, and dockyards. What the British Empire needs is three fleets

[1] A. Hurd and H. Castle, p. 374.

consisting of capital ships of moderate size, corresponding to the '74 of Nelson's day or the "Majestic" of 1900, able to go anywhere and do anything. Thirty "Majestics" cost no more than five "Hoods." Which class suits the needs of the Empire best ?

After the experiences of the last war it seems likely that a reaction will set in against a fleet of colossal ships ; for such a fleet implies a battle-line of immense length, difficult to handle and to keep in touch with an enemy, especially if he is bent on evading contact. Very rarely have big fleets come to a definite issue, as was seen at those elaborate fiascos, Beachy Head (1690), Malaga (1704), and Toulon (1744). The decisive battles have been those fought by fleets of moderate size, where commanders are not oppressed by a sense of overwhelming responsibility or of clogging bulk.

Further, the 15-inch or 16-inch gun implies a battle at very long range. But this is exactly the type of battle which always has been indecisive. Our great admirals have always inculcated closing with the enemy—witness Nelson's Trafalgar Memorandum of October 9, 1805 :

"In case signals can neither be seen nor perfectly understood, no captain can do very wrong if he places his ship alongside that of an enemy." [1]

Such were also the tactics of Rodney, Howe, and Hood. But the monster gun, as also the torpedo, render them impossible. Other disadvantages of such a gun are its short life, and therefore the costliness of gunnery practice, without which, however, rapid and efficient shooting cannot be attained.

To sum up : The feat of surprising the enemy's fleet has become more and more difficult owing to recent developments in scouting by aircraft and submarines, which by means of wireless can transmit news instantaneously to the Admiralty and the commander-in-chief. Therefore, unless under exceptional conditions like those which prevailed at

[1] Nicolas, vii. 91.

Jutland, it is very doubtful whether the weaker fleet will be caught unawares. If it is not so caught, no battle is likely to occur. Even if it is caught, escape is not difficult under cover of a smoke screen and a resolute charge by light craft. No victory is complete without pursuit ; but nowadays pursuit may be a fatal proceeding, destined to lead the fancied victor into a carefully prepared minefield. For these emergencies the increase of size in the capital ship is of no avail. Rather does it increase the magnitude of the losses resulting from unseen and incalculable dangers.

It would seem, then, that modern inventions have brought naval warfare to a state resembling deadlock ; and at present no way out is apparent. There is little hope of a solution along the lines lately followed by the three chief Admiralties of the world. Their solution of the problem is to arm their new battleships with 16-inch guns instead of 15-inch guns. What will be the result ? Of course, bigger ships, each costing well over £6,000,000 ; but also battles at longer range—with proportionately better chances for the enemy to escape, under cover of his light craft.

It is, however, encouraging to see that there are signs of a halt in the construction of these " super-Dreadnoughts." At the time of the recent launch of H.M.S. " Nelson," an announcement appeared in the " Times," that battleships of the " Nelson " and the " Rodney " class would probably be the last of that colossal type. This is not the place to discuss the problem of what is likely to replace the great ship. That is a matter for experts. I have tried merely to point out that great battle-fleets, like those which did not close at Jutland, are not likely to achieve a decisive result, and that naval warfare will probably resolve itself into a prolonged blockade, exerted in reality against the enemy's civil population.

## II

## THE INDECISIVENESS OF MODERN LAND WAR [1]

IN the new "Letters of Mr. Walter Page" (p. 166) there is clear evidence that Field-Marshal Sir John French, quite early in the war, believed that it would end in a stalemate. How he arrived at that forecast we are not informed ; but as to its general accuracy there can be little doubt. By October 1914 his acute mind discerned the disagreeable truth that, after the Germans made good their position on the line of heights north of the River Aisne, it would be extremely difficult to turn them out ; for the numbers and resources on both sides were so vast, and, on the whole, so well balanced, that a new type of static warfare had clearly set in. In short, mass-warfare was beginning.

Signs of some such a change had long been apparent. They are obvious in the last campaigns of Napoleon. The French Revolution was the mother of conscription. It endowed the French army with mass. The genius of Napoleon endowed that army with energy ; and the resulting momentum overthrew Old Europe. But it is the tendency of warlike action to beget a reaction of approximately equal strength. The democratic - national impulse in France, incarnate in Napoleon I., arouses equally strong forces successively in England, Spain, Prussia, Russia, and Italy. These nations embattle themselves against him. National armies spring from the soil in 1812–14 and finally

[1] Read to the Royal Institution on March 25, 1926.

by the weight of numbers gradually drive him back to Paris.

" Providence is on the side of the big battalions." Such is one of his most famous sayings. It is, perhaps, the falsest, for the lesson writ large on his career is that reliance on the big battalions finally raises in opposition an equal or even greater armed force. His grandiose efforts led to none of the results which he had in view, and they left France in a position politically weaker than that in which he found her.

But the later campaigns of Napoleon also illustrate my theme in a more technical sense, for they foreshadow one of the characteristics of the World War, namely, the increasing difficulty of reaching a decisive issue without a paralysing loss of life. It is curious to find one of Napoleon's generals afterwards complaining that most of his later battles were terribly sanguinary and yet disappointingly indecisive. This was the conclusion reached by General Rogniat in his work, " Sur l'Art de Guerre," published in 1817. After surveying the course of the Napoleonic campaigns, he ventures upon remarks which have a prophetic ring. Deprecating an excessive reliance on artillery, he maintains that the number of cannon should be in inverse proportion to the excellence of the troops. His argument is as follows : If a commander relies chiefly on artillery, he is tied to the good roads, for only on them can he advance his guns and his munition waggons. Also in the ensuing battle he mounts his guns so as to command the enemy's lines. The infantry merely supports the cannon. Accordingly, the engagement degenerates into an artillery duel at long range. The enemy, if he has the worst of it, has time to withdraw and to take up another position or else to retreat altogether. Little or no pursuit is possible, and the whole affair becomes (I quote his exact words) " a cruel game which wastes men's lives without results, and leads to an endless prolongation of the war." [1] Rogniat therefore censures the excessive reliance on artillery which generally characterised

[1] Rogniat, *op. cit.* p. 502.

Napoleon's later campaigns ; and he points out that these battles (especially those of 1813, when the Emperor rein-forced his levies of raw conscripts by large parks of artillery) wasted the lives of Frenchmen with little or no proportionate result.[1]  Equally emphatic was our military writer, Colonel Hamley, who wrote in 1866 : " Surplus artillery is far worse than useless : it hampers and delays the columns, destroys roads, perplexes generals, keeps troops out of action for its escort and protection, and impedes the retreat." [2]

Rogniat also criticised the use of dense masses of men in the later Napoleonic campaigns.  He pointed out that, from the Battle of Wagram onwards, the number of com-batants was often so great that no commander-in-chief could exercise effective control in the battlefield, not to speak of the difficulty of feeding them on the march.  For effective control and quick movement Rogniat placed the maximum of an army at 120,000 men.  If, says he, the enemy made use of vast masses, you could harass him by despatching light columns on his flanks to threaten his communications, and thus compel him to spread out, whereupon one of his corps could be cut off.  At the worst, the smaller army, being more mobile, could avoid a battle and thus gradually bring him into difficulties.  On his side, he could force you to a battle only by enveloping you by lightly equipped detachments ; but by so doing he would weaken his force and expose it to a blow at one of the wings.[3]

Rogniat's arguments against dense formations and large parks of artillery were in vain.  After 1860 the mania for masses revived and carried everything before it as against the small professional army.  In our own days the results of the American Civil War and of the Franco-German War seemed to justify the trust in huge numbers.  The triumph

---

[1] *Ibid.* 401-403.  He advised only 60 guns to a corps of 30,000 men as the maximum.  For Napoleon's criticisms see his " Correspondance," vol. xxxi. pp. 325-328.  Napoleon wanted 4 guns to every 1000 men (*Ibid.* p. 411).

[2] E. B. Hamley, " Operations of War," p. 395.

[3] Rogniat, pp. 245-247.

of Germany in 1870 was overwhelming ; and if we examine the causes of that triumph, we find them to resemble those which bore Napoleon I. to victory down to 1806, viz. masses of troops inspired by national enthusiasm, equipped with great thoroughness and led with consummate skill. Sedan is the counterpart of, and retort to, Jena.  A national army crunches up a smaller, badly organised, and ill-led professional army.

But note the sequel.  After 1870, all the neighbours of Germany are so impressed by her phenomenal successes that they too create national armies.  Except in these islands and the United States conscription becomes the rule.  Mass-warfare becomes the aim of every Continental War Office ; and just as Napoleon after 1810 finds himself confronted more and more by nations in arms, so too Germany after 1871 sees one nation after another conscript its manhood with the aim of attaining security.  Alliances and Ententes are formed for the same purpose ; and, after forty years of feverish competition in armaments and alliances, Germany finds herself relatively in no better a situation than when the race began.  By the year 1914 she has attained her maximum of military strength.  Her rivals, especially Russia, have not quite attained their maximum of military strength.  Therefore in 1914 war is the natural outcome of what is virtually a political and military deadlock.

The effect of huge armaments in producing war has been thus described by one who had the best possible opportunity of gauging their influence.  Viscount Grey in his book " Twenty-five Years " writes thus :

" Great armaments lead inevitably to war.  If there are armaments on one side there must be armaments on other sides.  While one nation arms, other nations cannot tempt it to aggression by remaining defenceless.  Armaments must have equipment ; armies cannot be of use without strategic railways.  Each measure taken by one nation is noted, and leads to counter-measures by others.  The increase of armaments, that is intended in each nation to produce consciousness of strength and a sense of security, does not produce these effects. On the contrary, it produces a consciousness of the strength of other nations, and a sense of fear. Fear begets suspicion and distrust and evil imaginings of all sorts." [1]

Prussia's huge armaments after 1861 were at first, I believe, honestly intended to be defensive. A generation later their evil results were apparent ; and in 1914 united Germany encountered great national armies on both fronts. Again, then, trust in the big battalions worked out its own retribution in the sphere of statecraft. Unhappily for the lives of millions, the political deadlock, which had been reached in 1913–14, was to be solved by four and a quarter years of wholesale slaughter, as against two years at the end of the career of Napoleon I.

The length of this struggle between the new Nation-States was certainly unexpected. No one had foreseen the persistence of the long-drawn-out agony into which Europe stumbled in August 1914. Every one had been impressed with the swift potency of modern weapons. What with aeroplanes for scouting, great guns firing high explosive, and howitzers that with one direct hit could wipe out a fort, the German High Command anticipated speedy triumph ; and if some churlish destiny delayed the accomplishment of the policy of Potsdam, there were held in reserve reservoirs of poison gas to hurry on the *dénouement*.

But what need of these adjuncts ? In themselves and by themselves the German hosts would dwarf the Sedan campaign both in speed and thoroughness. The Germans vaunted their army as a marvel of mobility. Motor traction of great guns, even of travelling kitchens, seemed to have solved the problems of transport and refreshment. Field telegraphs, field telephones, motor bicycles and special signal services kept the moving columns in touch with Headquarters, and imparted regularity to their advance. Further, when it came to a battle the same means of transmitting

---

[1] Viscount Grey, " Twenty-five Years," i. 91-92.

news promised to secure cohesion along a front of twenty
or thirty miles.  Gone were the days of galloping aides-de-
camp.  Orders now thrilled along field telegraphs or field
telephones.  Therefore the modern battle, like the modern
march, would be a matter of swift and overwhelming movement ; and wars would be won by a few mighty strokes.
Such were the forecasts.

The students of war who prophesied a short and decisive struggle in 1914 were reinforced by the economists,
who assured mankind that fighting could not long continue on a great scale, because bankruptcy and sheer exhaustion must inevitably and speedily ensue.  Nay ! there
were some cheery souls in the economic left wing who
proved to demonstration that a world war could not happen
at all.

Our leading soldiers did not foresee the character of the
war then imminent.  Lord Grey describes the bewilderment
of Lord Kitchener at the amazing development of trench
warfare on the western front.  "I don't know what is
to be done (he said to Earl Grey) ; this isn't war." [1]
The German High Command seem to have been equally
unprepared for the change.[2]

It was not a soldier, but a civilian who foresaw it.
M. Bloch, a Polish civilian, prophesied that modern inventions (quick-firing guns, high explosive, etc.) would
revolutionise war.  He pointed out that the effects of
artillery and machine guns were so deadly that flesh
and blood must evade them by some means, and would
probably take to trenches, as had happened at Sevastopol
and Plevna.  But M. Bloch was laughed at as a pacifist
whose wish was father to his thought.

Certainly the opening phases of the war seemed to belie
him.  Within six weeks of its beginning two great battles
had been fought, in which the invaders were heavily repulsed.  At the end of August the two Russian armies
invading Prussia got out of touch and were promptly

---

[1] Grey, "Twenty-five Years," ii. 69.

[2] Falkenhayn, "Critical Decisions at H.Q.," pp. 23, 35, 40.

punished by Hindenburg, who, with inferior forces but far superior strategy, defeated them in detail and with immense loss. Ten days later the German invaders of France over-reached themselves and exposed their right flank to a crushing blow from a new French army suddenly advancing from Paris. At bottom both defeats were due to an over-hasty and ill-concerted advance which exposed the invaders to condign punishment dealt out in true scientific manner. Optimists then deemed the end of the war not far distant.[1] For how could even great nations endure this terrific punishment ?

But then a strange thing happened on the western front. After the Battle of the Marne the beaten Germans retreated to the naturally strong line of heights which fringe the northern banks of the River Aisne and there defiantly faced about. Hastily digging trenches, they repelled the assaults of the Allies. These last, when reinforced, sought to outflank the now strongly fortified positions. But the Germans, ever strengthened from the rear, spread out so as to repel these flanking moves. By degrees, during the autumn of 1914–15, these efforts to outflank and to repel were extended to the north-west and the south-east. The move towards the north-west was the most fiercely con-tested. In fact it became (as Falkenhayn has termed it) a "race to the sea ". Certain authorities, both French and British, have claimed that the Allies should have hurried far more troops to the north-west, in which case Antwerp might have been held and the Germans kept away from the sea. Be this as it may, Antwerp for a time pinned a German force to that quarter. Ten days were thus gained, and by the end of October it was clear that the "line " would pass near Nieuport.

Desperate battles were fought for the possession of road centres or commanding ridges. On the side of the Allies, the most successful and glorious of these efforts were those of the British army to hold the positions around Ypres,

[1] On September 17, 1914, several British Staff officers expected the war to be over by Christmas (W. Churchill, " World Crisis," i. 281).

which were deemed essential for the defence of Dunkirk
and the Channel ports.  As we saw in the previous lecture,
the German High Command preferred military action
against the British army after it had landed to naval
action against it during the crucial time of crossing to
the Continent.[1]  Perhaps the German leaders erred.  They
should have done their utmost to destroy the British armies
at sea ;  or, failing that, to cut off its reinforcements
and munitions.  A German success at Ypres would have
involved the loss of Dunkirk, Calais, and Boulogne, of the
gallant little Belgian army behind the Yser inundations, and
the occupation of northern France as far as the lower course
of the River Somme.  The importance of the British success
at Ypres appears in the cautious words of Falkenhayn :

"The coast on which the [German] right flank was to
rest, and from which it was hoped to obstruct England's
Channel traffic, effectively attack the island itself, and turn
the French flank, was not reached."  [2]

Consequently the invaders had to be content with
holding the longer line northward to the River Yser.
However, at most points inland they were able to choose
commanding positions along the watersheds, so that their
front, when strengthened by all the resources of modern
science, held out against the utmost efforts of the Allies
during more than three and a half years.  Falkenhayn and
other German leaders have asserted that they disliked the
transition from open to trench warfare, that they adopted it,
first in the east, and then in the west, only "under the
stern pressure of necessity," because that method "once
more allowed full advantage to be taken of the interior
lines", and conferred freedom of action to strike where
necessary.[3]  Certainly their choice of the high ground right
away to the south-east as far as Lorraine was skilful,

[1] Falkenhayn (*op. cit.* p. 16) blames the German Naval Command
for refusing after the Battle of Heligoland (August 29) to risk "an
offensive into enemy waters."
[2] *Ibid.* p. 27.
[3] *Ibid.* pp. 40-42.

securing as it did a series of strong positions, which were rendered almost impregnable.

This phase of warfare was not altogether new ; for Wellington's occupation of the Lines of Torres Vedras had furnished a precedent. Between the Atlantic and the estuary of the Tagus above Lisbon he had entrenched and fortified a line of heights of great natural strength. His right wing, the most vulnerable part of his front, was covered by British gunboats so effectively that his opponent, Marshal Masséna, never seriously attempted to turn it. The Allied left, resting on the sea, was similarly protected. One point only near the centre was somewhat weak ; and that point Wellington strengthened by all the resources of the military art. There, behind these famous lines, he held at bay the best of the French Marshals and the best of the French troops, until famine and the winter rains starved out and rotted the invaders. In a military sense Torres Vedras pointed the way to the trench warfare of 1915–18.

But the later episode dwarfed the earlier ; and the German invaders had the advantage of living in the most fertile lands of France and Belgium. There is this further difference. Wellington always remained strictly on the defensive. He was victor if he did but hold his own. But the Allies in the recent war ran the risk of losing it if they could not drive the Germans from France and Belgium. So did the invaders unless they could pierce the defenders' lines. Therefore on the western front the deadlock was involuntary. Each side struggled hard to drive the other out. And yet neither side won more than local and temporary successes until the year 1918.

If we inquire into the reason for this almost complete deadlock, it would seem to be first, the increased ability of well-armed infantry to hold a considerable extent of front. A single line of steady well-trained men under moderate cover can, as was proved at the First Battle of Ypres, hold up large masses of assailants. This has been the characteristic British tactic ever since Wolfe first used the double line at Quebec in 1759. Wellington used it many times with deadly effect; and the introduction of the light quick-firing rifle has made this method of defence far more effective than ever. Given sufficient numbers of well-trained men, it is now possible to hold an extent of front never dreamed of before the time of the quick-firing rifle; and if you place them in well-protected trenches, you treble their defensive power.

But, secondly, infantry has come to depend more and more on artillery. The Germans did so especially. Mr. Winston Churchill wrote on October 8, 1914, as to "the absolute reliance of the Germans on their artillery, without which they would cease to be formidable." [1] Dependence on artillery and machine guns is no new feature; for during many years their development had outpaced that of the rifle. But in 1914–17 it baffled all prevision, so that for a time on all the fronts, and nearly to the end on the western front, warfare became for the most part a prolonged artillery duel. Concealed machine guns rendered attacks on the system of front trenches extremely costly; for in front of the trenches barbed wire entanglements held up the assailants; and night assaults generally failed amidst these obstructions, sometimes nearly 100 yards deep. Consequently, the chance of carrying even the first line was small, except by overwhelming numbers launched forward under cover of fog. By dint of immense and well-concealed efforts, if favoured by the weather, a success could be attained; but the difficulties of the assailants after breaking through increased with every mile of the advance.

Here we come to the weak side of artillery. It renders advance very slow. The transport of cannon, munitions, etc. in time of pursuit encounters endless obstacles, especially where the retreating enemy destroys the roads, as he always tries to do, so that, as a rule, the pursuit is clogged after a few miles. It was hoped that motor traction would expedite pursuit; but it rarely does, for the reason that the enemy's system of trenches (not to speak of the destruction of the ground by your own intensive bombardment) plays

[1] "World Crisis," i. 386.

havoc with all motor traction. In bad weather pursuit is now impossible.

Another reason for the failure effectively to pursue was the diminution of the cavalry arm. By the year 1917 few cavalry divisions remained on either side ; for they presented too easy a target for the quick-firing guns ; and the dismounted horsemen were needed to make good the fearful wastage in the trenches. Therefore no flood of cavalry burst upon the retreating enemy, as happened after Jena. In fact, it was soon proved, as in 1813, that an army which relies on artillery and is weak in cavalry cannot pursue with effect ; for the enemy, when driven from one position, has time to retreat and fortify another.

Various tactics were adopted to break the enemy's line. On the Allied side, at Neuve Chapelle, massed artillery fire was used on a comparatively short front to shake the enemy beforehand, and a rather narrow wedge of infantry was driven in. The effort failed before the German counter-attack.

A different method was tried by us at Loos and by the French in Champagne, namely in each case to make a broad but somewhat shallow breach in the enemy's line. His lines, however, were far too deep for these tactics to make a serious impression.

Afterwards the doctrine of " limited objectives " found favour. It was carried out in the Battles of the Somme in July 1916. Giving up the hope of a decisive break through at any one point, the Allies trusted to a series of steady advances of infantry behind a creeping barrage of intensive artillery fire. These advances were made, half by the British, half by the French, along a broad front of some fifteen miles. They brought about what was the longest (possibly with the exception of the Verdun *épopée*) series of battles ever fought by large masses of troops, from July 1st to the middle of November 1916. Considering the rawness of most of the British troops and the difficulties of the ground in front of them, fortified as it was with German skill and thoroughness, the successes gained were highly

satisfactory.  But they were dearly bought.  At no one
point did we penetrate into the hostile lines more than
seven or eight miles in those four and a half months ; and
our casualties exceeded 400,000.  The French in the
southern sector suffered less.  The enemy is supposed to
have lost 600,000 men.  He had been driven out of valuable
positions, but he still retained the important road centres
at Bapaume and Péronne.

Thus the Somme campaign revealed the character of
modern warfare.  Artillery and machine guns formed the
deciding factors, to which all tactics must conform.  To
escape their destructive fire, armies dug themselves in, and
when entrenched defied all but the heaviest of assaults.
The advances were made slowly behind creeping barrages,
and when positions had at last been painfully won, they
could be held only with the help of machine guns, or, if
possible, of artillery.  Owing to the diminution of cavalry
there was no pursuit worthy of the name ; and, as we saw in
the case of naval battles, without a prolonged and close
pursuit the fruits of victory cannot be garnered.

Already this exasperating deadlock had stimulated the
world's inventors to frenzied efforts for a solution.  The
first attempt was a characteristic German product—poison
gas.  Like all deadly surprises, it scored some initial success,
as on the slopes of Hill Sixty (on April 22, 1915).  Yet, so
soon as the Allies had invented an effective gas-mask, this
form of devilry was countered.  In fact, it was more than
countered.  In two ways nature helped to punish the
Germans.  I always thought them fools to introduce
poison gas, seeing that they were north-east of the line,
and the Allies were to the south-west.  On most days the
wind blew the stuff back into their trenches and kept ours
immune.  But also towards the close of the war they
suffered from lack of rubber.  The naval blockade cut off
their supplies of this essential, so that in 1918 very many of
their gas-masks were made of leather and proved to be
mere death-traps for the wearers.  Probably this was one
cause of the German collapse in that autumn.  The number

of German casualties due to gas warfare is not, I believe, fully known ; but probably it far exceeded those of the Allies. However that may be, it is fairly certain that the enemy lost more than he gained by this lethal device.

The next effort to effect a breach in the enemy's line was by means of a British invention—the tank, so called because it was not a tank. Designed in 1915, it was perfected by the summer of 1916, and first came into action on September 15, 1916, to clear the way for our infantry attacking the German lines near Delville Wood and the village of Flers, south-west of Bapaume. The site chosen was unfortunate, the ground being too rough, too shell-pocked, to give the new invention a fair chance. Of 49 tanks then employed, 17 stuck on the way, and only 9 advanced ahead of the infantry. One of these crushed in a German line of wire and then sat down in the enemy's trench, enfilading it, and finally securing 300 prisoners. Nine other tanks waddled behind the leading assailants and did good work in silencing nests of machine guns or compelling obstinate groups to surrender. What happened to the 14 other tanks is not stated.[1] This début was a little disappointing ; for half of the effect of such an invention is due to stupefying surprise ; and that did not happen till a few days later in an engagement near the former. Then a tank (a " female ") attacked a German trench soon after dawn, effected an entrance, and walked down, "the enemy surrendering freely " at the approach of this novel Bellona : 370 prisoners then surrendered to our supporting infantry.

In most conditions the tanks were a highly valuable asset. Without this help it is difficult to see how the Allies could have held their own on the western front, especially after the collapse of Russia. Then, during some months, the weight of numbers was heavily against them. Their forward moves, that of the French in Champagne, and of the British (with some French help) at the Third Battle of Ypres, resulted in little or no gain of ground and in frightful losses. The struggles around Ypres came to be as much

---

[1] J. F. C. Fuller, " Tanks in the Great War," pp. 55-57.

struggles against the elements as against man ; and the tanks often floundered helplessly or stuck fast in the seas of mud.[1]  The torrential rains of that summer and autumn told heavily against the Allies in Flanders : and the truth was brought home that man's utmost efforts can be paralysed by a mere touch of the finger of Nature.  Amidst the swamps of Flanders she fought both sides to a stand-still by November 6, 1917.  On that day, after frightful losses, the British and Canadians clutched at and won the village of Passchendael at the top of its bloodstained slope ; but human endurance had outrun its utmost limits.

A few days later tanks had a far better chance on the lighter soil and easier slopes in front of Cambrai.  There the surprise attack of November 20, 1917, was headed by a cohort of these monsters, which, moving through the murk at dawn, threw the Germans into an indescribable panic, the result being that our infantry effected an advance of 10,000 yards in twelve hours.  At the Third Battle of Ypres an equal advance took three months.[2]  The German counter-attack of the 30th, however, robbed us of most of the ground thus won, very many tanks being by this time disabled.  Finally, when the enemy had improved his field-gun tactics against tanks, these last often suffered heavily.  Nevertheless; in the closing battles of the war both Hindenburg and Ludendorff attributed British successes largely to the tanks,[3] which, though not fulfilling all the high hopes once placed in them, certainly proved to be the most successful military invention of the war period.  But suitable ground is essential to their effective use.

If time permitted, other military inventions might be mentioned which had some effect.  But I must now notice

[1] See Major G. K. Rose, M.C., " Story of the 2/4th Oxon. and Bucks. L.I.," pp. 126, 139, also for the deadly work of German machine guns. On pp. 55, 88, 204, he points out the clever moves of the Germans in evacuating their front lines and thereby for a time restoring open warfare.

[2] Fuller, " Tanks in the Great War," ch. 19.

[3] Hindenburg, " Out of my Life," pp. 390-392 ; Fuller, chs. 31, 34 ; A. Philipp, " Die Ursachen des deutschen Zusammenbruchs " (Berlin, 1925), p. 211.

an obvious objection. It is this. In the years 1917 and 1918 three breaches were effected, or almost effected, viz. at Caporetto in October 1917, opposite Bapaume in March 1918, and in Palestine in September 1918. Let us examine these cases in order.

Before his attack on the Italian line at Caporetto the enemy had found means to infect large numbers of the Italian troops in that sector with the notion that peace might be had for the asking. On the misty rainy morning of October 24, 1917, a picked German division, General von Bülow's, was launched at this morally weak point and crushed in the resistance of the loyal Italians. Their efforts were rendered futile by some disaffected units, from which men streamed out with white flags greeting their Teutonic " comrades," only to find themselves prisoners and treated with the contempt due to them. But their treachery was fatal, and the Austro-German lines swept on, compelling the Italians on both sides to loose their hold of the Alpine foothills and fall back into the Venetian plain. The ill-will of some and the panic of nearly all converted the retreat into a rout, which swayed on and on, beyond the Rivers Tagliamento and Livenza, and was stayed only behind the banks of the Piave (November 12). There, however, and on the Asiago plateau above the upper Brenta, Italy and her Allies held up the invaders, who, for all their phenomenal captures of men and material, wholly failed to break the will to fight of the Italian army and the Italian nation. This, the greatest disaster to the Allies during the whole of the war, was due chiefly to skilful propaganda among discontented Italian troops. Rightly considered, the sequel revealed the ability of a badly beaten army, when reinforced, to rally behind a moderately good physical barrier ; and it further revealed the solidity of the modern Nation-State. A new age had dawned since the days when a single defeat like Austerlitz or Jena could shatter a Government. Nowadays, mass must grind against mass for years to bring about, first a subsidence, and then a fall.

Still more instructive was the final failure of the Germans

to break the Allied line in northern France by the great offensive of March 1918. This is no place in which to criticise the British Government for its neglect to strengthen the weakest part of our line in front of Bapaume and Péronne. In spite of expert advice, that sector was left dangerously weak, though there were large numbers of new troops ready in England, and the German preparations for a great offensive were known. On the other side the German High Command prepared for a spring at our Fifth Army with as many as 44 divisions. After the completion of their preparations, they were favoured by a foggy morning, and then put forth a tremendous effort. Consequently General Gough's army was shattered and driven back beyond Albert, with the result of endangering the important railway centre, Amiens. The sequel is significant. In spite of all their initial successes the Germans failed to break the new defensive line hastily formed by the defence. The hills and villages west and south of Albert were held ; and the invaders' efforts there, as also up the Lys valley, came to a stand from sheer exhaustion.[1] They had badly shaken the Allies, but had not severed the British from the French as was their intention. Moreover, their losses were so heavy as to weaken them seriously for the final rounds in the summer and autumn, when the weight of the American armies began to tell. Therefore their spring offensive must be written down as a temporary tactical success, but, on the whole, a decided strategic failure. It did not effect a complete break through.

General Allenby's rupture of the Turkish lines in the Plain of Sharon belongs to a different order of things ; for it led to a crushing victory. There the element of surprise decided the immediate issue. The British commander, having gained complete mastery in the air, was able completely to outwit the Turks and their German advisers, skilfully inducing them to believe that his blow would fall on their left towards the Jordan, whereas he secretly countermanded the eastern movements of his troops by

[1] Hindenburg, p. 350-356.

day into a westerly concentration by night near to the
Plain of Sharon fringing the Mediterranean. Also from
behind the baffling screen of the sea there came at his bidding light cruisers to enfilade the Ottoman right flank.
On this his blow fell with telling effect ; and through the
breach there effected he poured a torrent of horsemen.
The result was a greater Jena. On successive days cavalry,
mounted rifles, and aircraft swept the Turks northwards,
then eastwards, across the Jordan, through Damascus, and
away far north to Aleppo.

What is the significance of this unexampled triumph?
Surely this, that the commander who has a decided superiority in aircraft and cavalry and succeeds quickly in
capturing the enemy's artillery, can not only break through
but also push on so far beyond as to decide the whole of the
campaign.[1] In other words, he can restore the war of
movement, for which some four millions of men were to the
very end struggling on the western front. At the climax
of the Palestine campaign metal did not outweigh man, as it
came to do in the European arenas. In the east the mobile
elements of warfare regained ascendancy over what may be
called the static elements, which produced almost a complete deadlock in the west.

By way of contrast with Allenby's campaign, consider
the closing phase of the war in France in the autumn of
1918. In the last resort it resulted from the arrival of
some 2,000,000 fresh Allied troops,[2] just as the reverses of
March were due to the decided superiority of German and
Austrian troops lately withdrawn from the eastern front.
In both cases, as between equally brave men, it was mass
that counted. The Allies, now having a marked superiority
in numbers, equipment, and *moral*, gained the upper hand

---

[1] Allenby's force apparently captured the Turkish artillery by the second
day, thus effecting what Haig and Byng hoped to achieve by cavalry
if they broke through completely at Cambrai on November 20, 1917.

[2] The American army in France increased from 4 divisions on
January 1, to 42 divisions on November 1 (Repington, " The World
War," ii. 467, 487). Though most of these were not sent to the front,
their presence as reserves had a great moral effect.

from August 8 onwards. As we have seen, tanks played a prominent part in these successful operations.[1] The tale of the German losses mounted with every week. Austria's final collapse on the line of the Piave was due, perhaps, as much to internal weakness as to the vigour of the Allied attacks ; and her surrender on November 3, following that of Bulgaria and Turkey, left Germany in a hopeless position. Between their first successes early in August and the Armistice, the 59 British divisions defeated the 99 thinner German divisions opposed to them, capturing 187,000 prisoners and 2,850 guns. The results achieved by the French, Belgians, and Americans were nearly as great. But the final cause of Germany's defeat was the eating up of her reserves. She could not now replace her terrible losses. In August 10 German divisions were broken up, and in October as many as 22. As the German official report on the collapse states : " The Reserves were exhausted " (*Der Ersatz ging zu Ende*).[2] On October 22 youths of eighteen were ordered to the front.

Nevertheless, as the pressure of the Allies was applied almost equally all along the huge front, no decisive rent was made. In fact, the Allies encountered increasing difficulties with every mile of the advance. Their progress was least in the most critical sectors, those in front of Verdun and the Argonne, where, largely owing to defects of the American transport, the progress ranged from about twenty-five miles to as little as six. Therefore the retreat of the Germans to the Rhine was not seriously threatened by November 11. The advance, which was greatest in the sectors in front of Château-Thierry and in that from the River Oise to Albert, led to a steady driving back of the whole hostile force, not to a *débâcle* at any decisive point, *i.e.* near their communications. These facts must be faced fairly and squarely. They amount to this, that after four and a quarter years the invaders were pushed back to

---

[1] K. F. Novak ("Der Sturz der Mittelmächte," p. 120), admits this.

[2] A. Philipp, pp. 208-211. The average strength of the German battalions sank during October from 545 to 450 men.

positions not far removed from those which they had
seized by the end of August 1914. But the Allies nowhere
got them decisively on the run. In fact, neither side could
move quickly, because clogged by artillery and heavy
transport and mud. For these reasons the war of movement was not restored in the west.[1]

The question whether it will ever be completely restored
in mass-warfare opens up a wide field of conjecture.
Despite all the recent efforts to introduce mechanicalised
transport so as to render armies more mobile, it seems
doubtful whether in a war where millions are embattled the
old mobility can be recovered, unless aircraft entirely revolu-
tionises the art of war. The outstanding lesson of the
World War is that every invention is speedily countered,
the result being for the most part a technical stalemate.
Further, during the Army Manœuvres of 1925 mechanicalised transport could not stand the strain of bad roads in
Hampshire resulting from a wet September. How, then,
is it likely to stand the strain of a winter campaign ? The
more mechanical the equipment of an army becomes, the less
is it likely to endure the prolonged wear and tear of war.[2]

It seems doubtful therefore whether modern warfare,
when waged on a vast scale, will escape from the deadlock
which gripped millions of men in 1915–18. The predomin-
ence of artillery seems to be likely to lead again to trench
warfare ; and when that stage is reached the struggle becomes one of slow attrition. The chief aim becomes not
so much the gaining of ground as the wearing down of the
enemy's man-power. In the old war of movement and of
small armies the butcher's bill was comparatively unim-
portant. Success turned mainly on the occupation of
crucial centres and dominating positions. These, of course,
still possess their value in war, but the vaunted progress of
the applied sciences and of the military art has, in effect,

[1] I cannot agree with Philipp that the Revolution brought about
Germany's collapse. He admits (p. 213) that before that time she had
lost the war.

[2] See General Sir W. Robertson's articles on the Army Manœuvres
in the " Morning Post," September 1925.

brought us back essentially to the time of tribal warfare, when tribe killed off tribe.  There is this difference : they did it in a few days : our war of attrition goes on for years ; and that side wins which most effectively grinds down the enemy's man-power and compels him finally to send boys of eighteen to the front.

It may seem impertinent for a civilian to venture on these criticisms of the military art ; but I have waited in the hope that some prominent admiral or general will speak out plainly as to the devastating deadlock to which modern warfare on a great scale has been reduced.  So far as I know, no one has done so.  Greatly daring, then, I have tried to point out that naval and military campaigns, when conducted with great masses and heavy artillery, lead to no proportionately decisive results.  At sea the introduction of the great gun and fire-control has been largely counterbalanced by the invention of wireless telegraphy and other devices, which enable the weaker fleet either to evade an action altogether, or at the desired time in a battle to slip away under cover of a smoke screen and a charge of their destroyers.  On land the dominance acquired by artillery and machine guns has led to all, and more than all, the clogging effects foretold by one of Napoleon's generals more than a century ago.  Human ingenuity has found means to elude the great shell and machine gun fire.  Men dig themselves in ; and warfare becomes, in essentials, a gigantic effort to dig them out.

Wearied by these long - drawn - out and ineffective struggles, inventors are turning their attention to the civil populations.  As fleets do not effectively grapple, submarines and aircraft are to assail merchantmen and cut off the needed supplies from oversea.  As armies only slowly wear each other down, aircraft are to pass them by and deal with the large cities—direct action with a vengeance.  These developments open up hideous vistas, unless mankind regains its sanity and comes to see that the whole ghastly business is a colossal farce.  The climax of scientific warfare proves, in practice, to be a *reductio ad absurdum*.

# III

## PLANS OF INVASION OF THE BRITISH ISLES

IT may be of interest to survey the chief plans of invasion
of these islands since the time of the advent of the sailing ship.  Raids on a small scale will not be considered; for
they are at all times possible to a daring enemy even if he
has small resources.  Invasions by a considerable force (say,
of 10,000 men or more) are different ;  for they imply the
desire to occupy territory, or the capital, and they involve
the use of a covering fleet.  The problem is therefore distinct from that of a raid which aims at local damage even
if it causes the loss of the attacking force.

Though the larger strategic issues of invasion remain
constant, yet important differences have arisen from developments in shipping and in the equipment of troops.  A
landing was easy in the primitive times when ships were
mere boats and soldiers could carry all needful weapons ;
when also the only means of warning the defenders were
beacon-fires.  It became increasingly difficult as ships
became larger, and field and siege artillery heavier ;  and
the problem took on a new complexion when the defenders'
scouts could telegraph by wireless the size and direction of
the attacking force.  England has enjoyed increasing im-
munity owing to these developments.  Her central position
off the coasts of North Europe would seem to invite a con-
centric attack from all the neighbouring shores, but no such
onset, though often. discussed, has ever been delivered.
Moreover the growth in the size of ships has told in her
favour.  From the time of Julius Cæsar to that of Philippe

le Bel the small oar-propelled craft of that age could muster in the cramped shallow harbours of Northern France or Flanders and easily land their hosts in south-east Britain.

Far different were the conditions in Tudor times when sea-going ships more and more displaced row-boats and galleys, whose two or three cannon firing straight ahead were overpowered by the broadside of a great sailing ship like the " Mary Rose." This was the outstanding lesson of the attempted invasion of Hampshire by Francis I.'s fleet of galleys and transports in 1545. Even in the calm waters of Spithead Henry's sea-going ships outmatched them, and still more in the battle off Shoreham.[1] It was then proved that a fleet of battleships at Spithead, lying to windward of the south-east coasts of England, rendered a landing on them impossible, unless the wind swung round persistently to the east.

The next forty years demonstrated still further the superiority of the broadside-ship to the galley, or even to the hybrid galleasse. And perhaps one of the reasons for English constructors concentrating on the sea-going ship was the perception that an invasion by galleys and pinnaces was formidable only when they were based on adjacent ports such as Boulogne, Calais, or Dunkirk, and that, even so, they must be covered by the enemy's sailing ships. Certainly, by the years 1585–87, Philip II. of Spain and his advisers decided that an invasion by an unprotected flotilla carrying troops from Dunkirk was out of the question. The best of Spanish seamen, Admiral Sta. Cruz, had urged Philip to invade England direct from Spain with a mighty force of 600 warships and transports acting independently of the Duke of Parma's army in the Spanish Netherlands. But Philip rejected this plan as far too costly ; and we may add it was probably far too cumbrous ; for it burdened the warships with a vast number of crowded transports, the whole mass having to run the gauntlet up the English Channel before a landing became possible. However that may be, he decided to utilise part of Parma's

[1] Corbett, " Drake and the Tudor Navy," i. pp. 50-59.

veteran army, which was to embark on transports collected
in the then shallow harbours of Dunkirk and Nieuport, and
meet the Spanish convoying fleet off the coast of Kent.

Here, then, we note the growing complexity of invasion
schemes, which almost inevitably depended on the protection of a flotilla of transports collected near the English
coast by a sea-going fleet.  There being no good deep-water
harbours between the mouth of the Scheldt and Brest, the
enemy must bring such a fleet from the Bay of Biscay into
the English Channel, whose narrowing wristlet exposes him
to an attack off a lee shore by the English fleet pursuing
from Plymouth or Portsmouth.  For Philip the matter
was worse, his nearest large harbour being Lisbon ; and
to co-ordinate the moves of great ships sailing thence with
the Flemish flotilla presented grave difficulties, which increased when Drake in April 1587 swooped on the main
part of the Armada at Cadiz, inflicted immense damage,
and demonstrated the superiority of broadside ships to
galleys, even in a harbour.  So despondent was Admiral
Sta. Cruz, commander of the Armada, that on November 4,
1587, he wrote to Philip : " . . . As to the issue of an
engagement in the open sea, or the possibility of seizing a
port, or the chances of effecting a landing, I do not think
we can count on them." He adds that, if any disaster befell
the Armada, it could not be replaced for a long time ; and
that the best policy was to hold it out over Elizabeth *in
terrorem* so as to induce her to " restore " Holland and
Zealand to Spain.[1]

Philip, however, was inflexible.  Believing that half of
England, and nearly all the Scots and Irish, would rise
against Elizabeth if a Spanish army landed in the Thames,
he decided to run great risks before landing.  (We may
note that nearly all invasion plans have rested on similar
assumptions, with results fatal to the contrivers and their
sympathisers in these islands.)  Philip, then, pushed on the
preparations, which, however, Drake's *coup* utterly dis-
arranged until the summer of 1588.  Meanwhile Parma's

[1] Calendar State Papers, Venetian (1581–91), pp. 320-322.

flotilla rotted, and the crews sickened.   Another blow to
Philip was the death of his experienced admiral, Sta. Cruz.
Thereupon he appointed as commander of the Armada,
the Duke of Medina Sidonia, despite the pathetic protest of
the latter—" I know by the small experience that I have
had afloat that I soon become sea-sick and have many
humours." [1]  Nevertheless, Philip ordered that nervous
landsman to disregard any further efforts of Drake, and
make straight for the English Channel in order off " Cape
Margate " (the North Foreland) to join Parma's transports
from Nieuport and Dunkirk.   He will proceed thither if
possible without a battle so as to " keep your forces intact."   If, however, the English approach him, he may
fight them ;  they will try to fight at long distance ;  the
Spaniard must try for close quarters in order to board.   If
storms occur, he will consult what shelter to take.   A
" secret " postscript allows him, in case of failure, to seize
the Isle of Wight.[2]   In these instructions we hear the
ground-tone of continental strategy, which lays the first
stress on caution and the preservation of the fleet for
ulterior military ends.   Medina Sidonia, like Sta. Cruz
before him,[3] is, if possible, to keep his fleet intact in order
to guard the rear of the conquering Spanish soldiery.
Philip, apparently, did not see the need of beating the
enemy's main fleet before attempting a landing.   In his
view the Armada was a means partly of transporting,
partly of covering, the invading army.[4]

Equally determined were the English leaders to meet
it at sea.   At their head was now Lord Howard of Effing-
ham, Lord High Admiral, who, though less expert in naval
affairs than Drake, Hawkins, and Frobisher, came thoroughly to agree with them as to the need of attacking the
Spaniards on their own coasts.   In mid-June, 1588, that is,

---

[1] Calendar State Papers, Spanish (1587–1603), p. 207.

[2] *Ibid.* pp. 245-250.

[3] *Ibid.* pp. 186-188.

[4] See " The Fugger News-Letters " (2nd series), pp. 147-154 for a
Spanish view of the certainty of victory of the 170 Spanish ships over
the 40 English.

two months after he and his force joined Drake's western
fleet at Plymouth, he wrote to the statesman, Walsingham :
" It is hard matter and a thing impossible [for] us to lie in
any place or to be anywhere to guard England, Ireland, and
Scotland " ;  and he cited his experienced captains as
holding " that the surest way to meet with the Spanish
fleet is upon their own coast, or in any harbour of their own
and there to defeat them." [1]   Walsingham's chief difficulty
was to reconcile the Queen to this bold strategy ; for she
had bidden him order Howard " to ply up and down in some
indifferent place between the coast of Spain and this
realm "—a feminine half-measure which represented only
a slight strategical advance on her pettish outburst in
January :  " My ships have left to put to sea ; and if any
evil fortune should befall them, all would be lost ; for I shall
have lost the walls of my realm." [2]   Now, at midsummer
she at last conceded to Walsingham that Howard, whom she
believed a safe man, should decide ;  and he was now of
Drake's and Hawkins' opinion. [3]   So hard was it to ensure
that boldly prudent strategy which has since been the
bed-rock of English naval policy.

Yet the incalculable factor in naval warfare now inter-
vened to mar a wise plan.  The favouring northerly
breezes that bore Howard and Drake almost within sight of
Galicia veered to a stiff sou'-wester which drove them back
to Plymouth with depleted stores.  Swept along in the
skirts of the gale came the Armada.  Rallying stragglers off
Scilly, it ploughed along off the Cornish coast while Howard
and Drake were in harbour hurrying on their scanty refit.
What an opportunity !  Medina Sidonia had the three advantages longed for by a leader—readiness, the windward
position, and plenty of sea-room.  Hauling his wind before
opening Plymouth Sound, he might then have attacked the
English ships as they beat out against the wind to the open.

[1] " Defeat of the Spanish Armada " (N. R. Soc.), ed. by J. K. Laughton
(London, 1894), i. pp. 196, 200.

[2] Calendar State Papers, Spanish (1587–1603), p. 191.

[3] Read, iii. 305-307.

He let slip the opportunity.   Was it because his instructions discouraged fighting and prescribed first and foremost a junction with Parma's transports between Dunkirk and Margate ?   We do not know.   But in that hour, when nearing the Eddystone, the Duke lost the best chance of crushing the English people.   The brief reference in Howard's letter of July 21 gives a glimpse of his feelings at this crisis.   "We did what we could to work for the wind, which [by this] morning we had recovered." [1]   That is all.   But it enables us to picture the English fleet hurrying out, half-provisioned, tacking against the south-west wind, creeping past Penlee Point, and finally gaining the windward position.

This decided the issue.   Some 45 English warships, heavily armed, also faster and handier than any of the Spaniards, were now able to gall their rear in a long running fight, during which the Armada lost three of its best ships. Still the great mass, though badly shaken, held on eastwards.   "Their force is wonderful great and strong" (wrote Howard to Walsingham on July 29) "and yet we pluck their feathers little by little." [2]   In reality the defensive tactics of Medina Sidonia involved defeat.   A week of retreat, with little or no counter-attacking, sapped the *moral* of his crews ;  and his 100 tall ships, which, on July 28, anchored in the open roads of Gravelines, west of Calais, were a beaten force.   Howard and Drake, now joined by Seymour with the squadron from the Downs, dropped anchor to windward.   The one aim of the Duke had been to establish contact with the army of invasion ready to embark at Dunkirk and Nieuport.   But now he saw failure ahead.   In that wind-swept, tide-swept, roadstead he wrote to Parma that, as the English were on his flank, able to bombard him, while he could not reply, the transports must come out, and 50 fly-boats must come on to protect the great ships, for which it was imperative to find shelter.   He added these words :  "The general opinion is

---

[1] "Defeat of Armada," i. 288.
[2] *Ibid.* i. 341.

that it will be very inadvisable for the Armada to go beyond this place." [1]

Before this desponding appeal reached Parma, Howard at midnight of July 28–29 sent in against the Armada eight fireships. As they came in before the westerly wind on the flood tide, Medina Sidonia was seized with fear that they might have on board " artificial machines," and he gave orders to cut cables, himself setting the example. Thereupon the jostling mass drifted out to sea, bravely re-forming at dawn for a last effort. It went decisively against the Armada, which retreated into the North Sea, the English pursuing.

Meanwhile, a Dutch squadron had helped Seymour and Wynter maintain watch over Parma's expeditionary force.[2] In reality there was little need of a blockade ; for in several letters Parma complained that his craft were little better than river boats and were totally unable to beat out of Dunkirk against the prevalent westerly winds—" This wind " (he wrote to King Philip) " would prevent our boats from coming out, even if the seas were clear of the enemy's ships." And again " the set of the wind was such as to prevent even ships specially constructed for navigating these waters." [3]

Philip and Medina Sidonia were unaware of this disability. The latter had confidently expected to meet Parma's force off Margate, " without causing me to wait a minute " ; while in point of fact that harassed leader could not stir without a strong convoying force and light favourable airs. Parma was soon to be blamed for the failure of the whole enterprise ; whereas all the three landsmen wholly underrated the difficulty of the problem before them. Essentially it was this : how to bring a powerful sea-going fleet from Spain to the shoal-screened coast of Flanders and then from the shallow harbours, facing north-west, help a flotilla to struggle out and across

---

[1] Calendar State Papers, Spanish (1587–1603), pp. 358, 362, 363.
[2] " Defeat of Armada," ii. 49.
[3] Calendar State Papers, Spanish (1587–1603), pp. 366, 371, 383.

to England in the teeth of the prevalent westerly winds.
To co-ordinate the movements of a great fleet coming from
the Bay of Biscay and a cumbersome ferry is never easy
in the best of weather, and in succession, Louis XIV.,
Louis XV., and Napoleon were to fail, perhaps as much
owing to the inherent difficulties of the task as to the
efficiency of the English opposition.

We must pass quickly over the brilliant raid of the
Dutch into the Medway in 1667 ; for they possessed too few
troops to attempt a landing even in the unprepared England
of Charles II.   Equally fortunate were we in the summer
of 1690.   At that time the situation uniquely favoured
a resolute invader.   Englishmen had begun to dislike
William III., who was then in Ireland.   The Navy and
Army were honeycombed with Jacobitism, which might
prove overpoweringly strong if William were defeated in
Ireland and the Navy lost command of the Channel.
William made good at the Boyne ; but the Anglo-Dutch
fleet suffered a serious reverse off Beachy Head.   Torrington, however, skilfully retired behind the Gunfleet Shoal,
south of Harwich, where his " fleet in being " imposed on
the victorious French.   Tourville, though dominating the
Channel, and to windward of Torrington, made no attempt
at a landing ; and the most favourable opportunity vouch-
safed to an invader since the year 1066 passed away never
to return.   The vagueness of French plans and the irre-
solution of Tourville lost both the campaign and the
war.

Limiting our survey to considerable efforts at invasion
which were actually attempted, we now concentrate on the
episode of 1759.   The prospects of the French forcing a
successful landing were then by no means desperate.   True,
they, with their Allies Austria and Russia, had failed since
1756 to break the power of Great Britain and Prussia.   At
sea France had sustained heavy blows, while the surrender
of Louisbourg with her North American squadron (July
1758) portended the loss of Canada.   But in order to save
that colony the new Minister, the duc de Choiseul, planned

an invasion of Scotland, with subsidiary raids on England.
Early in 1759 he sought hard to secure the active naval
support of Russia, and, if possible, of the Swedes, who
resented the English maritime code. Further, as the
Anglophile King of Spain, Ferdinand VI., was slowly dying,
and his successor, Charles, openly favoured the French
cause, Choiseul cherished the hope of forming a great
maritime league against England. In Scotland, too,
Jacobitism was far from moribund ; and if Prince Charles
headed a French army landing in the Firth of Clyde, and
were joined by forces of Russians and Swedes landing at
Leith, the throne of George II. might be so shaken as to
loosen the British grip beyond the seas. If that was the
outcome of the prince's venture with six companions in
1745, what might not happen now if he headed 20,000
French, 10,000 Russians, and 10,000 Swedes at Edinburgh ?
In order to spread panic in England large bodies of troops
were echeloned on the coasts of Normandy and Flanders,
ready to cross over in flotillas of flat-bottomed boats. A
small squadron was also prepared at Dunkirk to sail along
the east coast of England and Scotland, spreading alarm,
and drawing off our warships in pursuit.[1]

Pitt was not flustered. Early in the war he received
information on the highest authority that the French War
Minister, Belleisle, would invade England with a small force
" only in case of extremity, as he looked upon it as most
dangerous and desperate."[2] Further, the experience of
former attempts at invasion warranted confidence. Like
all our experienced seamen, he knew from the events of
1588 onwards that the hostile flotillas depended on the
support of their fleets ; and it was probably in order to
assuage public excitement that he and Anson sent Rodney
to bombard the flotilla at le Havre.

On the contrary, Choiseul seems to have believed in all
portions of his grand design. In politics imagination is a
good servant but a bad master ; and the duke strove

---

[1] Hannay, ii. 176-179.
[2] " Correspondence of Earl of Chatham," i. 208.

desperately to co-ordinate these far-flung schemes and fit them in with the facts of naval warfare.  His great enemy at London, equally imaginative, but also practical, saw that this complex machinery of invasion would not start until it received the needed impulse from the French fleet ; and after its losses at Louisbourg and in both the Indies, that marine was barely equal to the blockading forces which the vigour of Pitt maintained in high efficiency off Brest and Toulon.  As that statesman discerned the outlines of the French scheme he in mid-May despatched Hawke with the Channel Fleet to observe Brest, while Boscawen kept a more distant vigil off Toulon.  A small squadron was also posted off Quiberon Bay to watch the crowd of transports there assembled under a small escort of warships.  For the original French design was that, while the Brest fleet under Conflans dealt with Hawke's main body, the Quiberon transports and escort would put to sea, beat off the British light squadron, and then make for Scotland *via* the west of Ireland.

As usual, the French opened the game in the Mediterranean ; but now under less favourable conditions than in 1690–92.  William III. and his counsellors had then discerned the supreme need of a naval base, or bases, in the Mediterranean.  In 1704, Gibraltar, and in 1708 Minorca, fell to the British arms ; and though in 1756 the moral cowardice of Byng lost the latter stronghold, yet the watchfulness of Boscawen now partly made up for that deficiency.  Forced to retire from before Toulon to Gibraltar to refit, he was there warned betimes by his scouting frigate that the French fleet was bounding along on an easterly gale for the strait.  Hastening after the enemy, by good management and good luck he caught them while scattered between Cadiz and Cape St. Vincent (August 17, 18, 1759).[1]  The result was utterly to mar the favourite French gambit, and leave the Brest fleet unequal to the real or potential blockading force.  Thus, once again, as in 1692, the partition of the French Navy between the Mediterranean and Ocean

[1] Corbett, " England in the Seven Years' War," ii. 32-39.

was fatal to the concentration which alone could bring success in northern waters.

Nevertheless, Choiseul clung to his scheme, and, despite the approach of autumn, ordered the Quiberon force with its escort to put to sea at the earliest opportunity. " Sweden is waiting for us (he wrote on October 3) : I fear that she will not wait long, and that the decisive moment will be past if you do not start by the end of this month." For diplomatic reasons, then, Choiseul forced on the invasion plan.

But now it underwent a change   Admiral Conflans strongly urged that all the French warships at Brest and Quiberon should re-unite, in order, with at least 21 sail, to attack Hawke's fleet of about the same number. Then, after driving him away, the French would fall upon any British warships off Quiberon, and escort the French transports to the Firth of Clyde. The change was approved by Louis XV. in council.[1] Indeed, concentration was now essential, if Conflans was not to be crushed at the outset.   Yet the change had this disadvantage, that it left the French transports unprotected in Quiberon Bay, and also compelled Conflans to proceed thither at the earliest opportunity.   This he did in a stormy spell in mid-November when Hawke was obliged to shelter in Torbay. Driven west for a time by squalls from the south-south-east, Conflans on November 20 (when the wind veered sharply to north-west) sighted the British light squadron keeping watch off Quiberon.   But while he prepared to entrap it, he was himself threatened by Hawke's 23 sail heaving in sight to the west of Belleisle, driving along at full speed for the same destination.

To describe the ensuing Battle of Quiberon Bay would be superfluous.   What concerns us is the faultiness of the French plan.   Its fundamental defect was the assemblage

[1] R. Waddington, "Guerre de Sept Ans," iii. p. 367.   This explains surely what Colomb ("Naval Warfare," p. 148) thought mysterious, viz. why Conflans made for Quiberon.   As Hawke was thought to be far away, Conflans' own modification of the original plan compelled him to proceed to Quiberon to start the invasion scheme.

of the army of invasion around a bay distant some 100 English miles from the convoying fleet at Brest. This introduced a needless complexity and made it practically certain that the Brest fleet, after a sortie, would proceed to that bay. Therefore Hawke, after losing Conflans' fleet, naturally directed his course thither,[1] with the result that the French fleet and many transports were destroyed or scattered, and the whole plan upset. It is needless to add that the Russians and Swedes never stirred. Also Charles III. of Spain, on hearing news of the French disaster at Quiberon, explained away the rather threatening demands he had begun to proffer to the British Court. The dependence of delicate diplomatic arrangements on the hard facts of naval warfare could not be better illustrated than by the collapse of Choiseul's grandiose but unsound scheme. Pitt and Anson checkmated it by keeping fast hold on the hostile fleets from the start. This course of action, aimed at by Drake in 1587, was again and again to prove England's sheet anchor in time of danger.

This essay would be unduly prolonged if every scheme of invasion were noticed ; and few comments seem called for on that of 1779. After the addition of France in 1778 and of Spain in July 1779 to the ranks of our enemies, England was overmatched, her fleet being also in a wretched condition under the corrupt and inefficient administration of Lord Sandwich. The American War and the campaigns in the East and West Indies imposed so serious a strain on our naval resources as to leave us dangerously weak in the Channel, where the antiquated defences of Plymouth and Portsmouth invited a home thrust. In July 1779, when a large but ill-equipped Spanish fleet was about to join that of Brest, George III. issued a proclamation instructing farmers on the south coast to drive horses and cattle inland and by other means hinder the expected invaders. Booms and obstructions were also prepared at Plymouth and other ports, as was only natural when the Bourbon Powers sent forth 66 sail-of-the-line and had troops and transports ready

[1] Corbett, ii. pp. 53 ; Hannay, ii. p. 187.

along the coasts of Brittany and Normandy. Their first scheme was to seize the Isle of Wight and Portsmouth, but Spain preferred joint action against Gibraltar. The weak Louis XVI. could not frame any decided plan of action, but advocated an attempt on the English coast.

Meanwhile the Admiralty dragged out of retirement Admiral Sir Charles Hardy and placed under him 35 of the line, with general instructions (July 29) to put to sea and guard a valuable convoy from the westward, as well as prevent an invasion. It would seem that Hardy regarded the former duty as more important than the latter ; for he cruised some thirty to sixty miles west-south-west of the Scilly Islands, thereby exposing Plymouth to grave danger from the great Franco-Spanish fleet, under Orvilliers and Cordova, which on August 16 lay becalmed and anchored off that port. Fortunately, weather conditions, the inability of that cumbrous force in any conditions to manœuvre, and the frequent changes of plan at Paris hampered its action. By a curious chance the Allies never closed with Hardy ; but their movements were ever clogged by the knowledge that he was to windward. Finally the alarming spread of pestilence on their Armada compelled it to return to port.

The only point of interest in this lumbering attempt is the dominant influence exerted by the smaller British fleet cruising to windward. That Hardy was much too far to the west is clear : his proper cruising ground was south of the Lizard, where he could effectively cover Plymouth ; but, even when west of the Scillies, he paralysed the numb energies of a seemingly overwhelming Armada.[1]

In singular contrast to the feeble action of Louis XVI.'s Government in 1779 was that of the Revolutionists who leaped to power in 1792. After declaring war on England and Holland on February 1, 1793, they prepared for

---

[1] Colomb, "Naval Warfare," 150-156 ; W. M. James, "The British Navy in Adversity," ch. 12 ; Chevalier, "Hist. de la Marine française," i. 157-173. See Kempenfelt's criticisms of Hardy in "Barham Papers" (N.R.S.), i. 292-299.

invasion, counting on active support from their sympathisers in these islands, especially Ireland. Admiral Palliser regarded their schemes as visionary except " by the assistance of rebellion, treachery and massacres." He, however, foretold that if the French conquered Holland, the risk of invasion thence would be greatly increased.[1] This danger materialised in 1795 when the new Batavian or Dutch Republic became allied to France, while in October 1796 Spain declared war. These events reduced us to the defensive and led *inter alia* to the abandonment of the Mediterranean so as to meet the danger nearer home. The enemy meanwhile projected invasions or raids from the French, Flemish, or Dutch ports; while General Hoche pointed to Ireland as certain to rise if even a small army landed. Ulster, then the most discontented province, was the favoured objective ; but the harbours of the south-west attracted the seamen, who also urged that feints be made from Picardy and Flanders to distract and terrify the English. The plan of an Indian expedition, long toyed with, was also deferred in order to concentrate on Ireland.[2]

The decision, though belated, was judicious ; for the appearance in Ireland of even a small French army under General Hoche, would have aroused the population and swept away British ascendancy. If 1100 French troops under General Humbert, landing after the failure of the Irish Rebellion of 1798, could penetrate from Killala to the heart of the island, what might not 14,000 troops under Hoche have achieved in 1796 ? After losing Ireland, England would soon have been exposed to invasion on her vulnerable west coast, a danger which from the days of Elizabeth to William III. she had struggled desperately to avert. Nerved by these hopes, the French Directory assembled at Brest some 14,000 troops, which were to be conveyed across by 16 sail-of-line, 14 frigates, and a few transports, the warships being packed with troops so as to

---

[1] " Spencer Papers " (N.R.S.), ii. 240-261, and 274-305.
[2] Desbrière, " Projets . . . de débarquement aux Îles Britanniques," 71-95, 117-152.

economise in transports. Wolfe Tone and several United
Irishmen were to sail with them and rouse Ireland, for
which purpose many thousand muskets were taken. In
order to evade the British fleet watching Brest, Admiral
Morard de Galles proposed to slip out by the little-used
Raz channel into the Bay of Biscay, sailing south-west by
south before putting about for the Irish coast.[1]

The plan possessed several merits. (1) It relied largely
on surprise and on the secrecy which could be observed on
short days ; (2) No time would be lost in sailing elsewhere
for transports ; (3) The feints to be made at other parts of
the British coast (*e.g.* that which belatedly stumbled on
Fishguard) would be likely to confuse the British Admiralty
as to the real objective ; (4) A landing in force anywhere
on the Irish coast would be likely to succeed ; for local help
would render the invaders largely independent of supplies,
even if the British fleet soon cut their communications with
France.

That the plan miscarried was due chiefly to accidents.
Morard de Galles got away from Brest on December 16 near
the end of an easterly gale which had driven far into
the Atlantic Admiral Colpoys' blockading fleet. But the
French lost this initial advantage owing to a sudden change
of wind to the south-east. Morard, when half through the
Raz Channel, therefore signalled to cease tacking against
the wind and run north-west towards the open. In the
gathering dusk great confusion ensued, and one sail-of-line
was lost with all hands. The Armada never recovered from
this dislocation ; and owing to rough weather made the
coast of Munster in scattered sections, none of which effected
a landing. For this inactivity, prolonged during nearly a
fortnight, the blame lay largely with the military men,
notably General Grouchy, who required impossible things
from the seamen in Bantry Bay.[2] Finally, as the Irish did
not rise, the scattered force dribbled back to Brest, losing
near there another valuable unit. Still, the fact remains
that, owing to mistakes of the British fleet off Brest, and

[1] *Ibid.* pp. 155-167.          [2] *Ibid.* p. 200.

the extreme slowness of sending to Portsmouth news of the French sortie, the invading force long lay unmolested on the coast of Munster, and even in its disorderly retreat never met more than a few British frigates. Well might the Opposition censure the Admiralty and Admirals Colpoys and Lord Bridport for faulty dispositions which endangered the public safety.[1]  Well might Wolfe Tone write that England had never had so narrow an escape.

The criticism may be urged that Hoche's invasion plan ignored British naval supremacy and aimed merely at evading it.  The objection is valid in nearly all cases ; but the case of Ireland was wholly exceptional.  There the chief consideration was the landing of a solid expeditionary force and the arming of the almost wholly malcontent population.  In such a case, if enough munitions could be landed, the loss of communications with France would be immaterial.  The real causes of failure were the confusion at the start, the further scattering in the bad weather which ensued, the parcelling out of the force from Bantry Bay to the Shannon, subsequent discords between soldiers and sailors, and utter loss of confidence on the part of the Irish.

Nevertheless the French Directory in the year 1797 by no means renounced the Irish scheme.  When the Spanish Mediterranean fleet moved northwards towards Corunna, it was with the aim of furthering an invasion of the British Isles, probably Ireland ; and the same guiding motive prompted the orders from Paris in October that the Dutch fleet must put out and join the French down Channel.  In these cases the British Admirals were equal to the emergency, the results being the battles off Cape St. Vincent and Camperdown.  Why in the intervening months the French did not utilise the priceless opportunity of the Mutinies in the Channel and Nore Fleets is a mystery which is only half solved by the far-fetched argument that an attack then would drive the mutineers back to duty.[2]  The fact remains that the enemy did not attack until October, when

[1] " Parliamentary History," vol. xxxiii. pp. 12-14, 109-115.
[2] Desbrière, i. p. 258.

even the Nore scoundrels were full of fight ; that in April-May 1798, under the influence of Bonaparte, the Directory took up again the Egyptian chimera, and thenceforth sent over to Ireland only driblets just sufficient to induce brave men to sacrifice themselves for nought.[1]

Meanwhile great flotillas of light craft were built at all the ports from Antwerp to Nantes, as if for the invasion of England.  In February 1798 Bonaparte advised against the plan as very dangerous so long as the British fleet held the seas, but he urged the continuance of the invasion menace so as to prevent our acting in the Mediterranean. In July 1801 the vastness of the French and Dutch flotillas induced the Earl of St. Vincent, then First Lord, to place Nelson in command of the coastal defence preparations. Our great seaman at first believed that the French would attempt a landing in West Kent or East Sussex, while their Flemish and Dutch forces would make for Essex or Suffolk.  Five weeks later, even after the failure of his attack on the Boulogne flotilla, he believed that they would not get half-way across.  Thus he came to the conclusion of Drake and many other Britons, that a flotilla alone was helpless, and that invasion implied at least a temporary command of the sea by the enemy's fleet.[2]

Napoleon's schemes of invasion being treated in the sixth essay, only a brief summing up need be attempted here.  It is clear that he learnt much from the earlier plans of Choiseul and the French Directory.  But, like them and Philip II. of Spain, he underrated the essential difficulty— that of co-ordinating the work of the fleet coming from the deep-water harbours of the ocean with that of the flotilla assembled in the shallow harbours of North France and Flanders.  For a time, apparently, he believed that that flotilla could fight its way across unsupported.  Realising by degrees the probability of disaster in such a case, he designed ingenious plans for evading or decoying away the British fleets watching Brest and Toulon.  Here again the

---

[1] Desbrière, ii. pp. 29-130.

[2] Sir H. Nicolas, " Despatches of Nelson," iv, 426, 500.

fundamental strategic defect of France hampered him.
Thanks to our base at Gibraltar (reinforced since 1800 by
that at Malta) he could never unite the Toulon and Brest
fleets ; and therefore could never convoy the flotilla across.
For a time early in August 1805 (as I have shown on
pp. 115-120) he came within sight of possible success ; but
the difficulties were too great for any but a French Nelson
to surmount ; and such a man he never found.

We may, perhaps, conclude somewhat as follows.   The
only really serious crises were those which arose when for a
time our fleets lost command of home waters, when also an
active and resolute enemy mustered within easy striking
distance considerable forces ready to embark on seaworthy
transports.   I submit that these conditions, *sine qua non*,
rule out the hostile efforts of the years 1588, 1596, 1667,
1745, 1756–59, 1797–1801 and 1803–05, with the possible exception of a few days early in August 1805 when Napoleon's
chances of invading England were favourable.   Only in the
years 1690, 1779, and 1796 had our enemies achieved the
conditions essential for success, namely, temporary (if
partial) command of the neighbouring seas and the ability
to transport across them a formidable military force.

The problem of home defence shifted somewhat after
1900, when the German navy rose rapidly to strength and
efficiency ; for, as Palliser and others had pointed out,[1]
the mouth of the Thames and the long accessible east
coast are our danger points ; and these Germany directly
menaced.   On the other hand her threatened supremacy
both on land and sea helped to unite with us France and
Russia.   Further, her sea base was so narrow as to render
the task of watching her fleet far easier than it was of yore
when our squadrons had to observe the extensive coasts of
France, with those of Spain and Holland often superadded.
From the time of Drake onwards the master-aim of British
seamen has been to defend England by observing the
enemy's chief naval bases.   It was therefore a great gain
when, in place of Brest, Rochefort, and Toulon (often with

[1] " Spencer Papers," ii. 240-261, 274-305.

Corunna, Cadiz, and Carthagena superadded), our seamen could concentrate their attention almost entirely on Wilhelmshafen and the mouth of the Elbe. The ability of Great Britain and France to block access to the English Channel and to render exceedingly difficult the northern exit from the North Sea was another important factor in the World War, similar to that which determined the issues of the Dutch Wars. The advent of the submarine also rendered highly dangerous the transport of a German army across the North Sea ; and, as I have pointed out, the increase in the *impedimenta* of an army has greatly increased the difficulty of landing except where quays and cranes abound. For these reasons, reinforced by the lessons of three centuries of naval warfare, it is not easy to see why in the recent war our Government considered an attempt at invasion by 70,000 Germans as not unlikely, and kept back considerable forces to repel it. On this topic an authority worthy of all respect, Field-Marshal Sir William Robertson, has written :

" The truth is that, however bravely one may talk in time of peace, when brought up against the grim proposition of an enemy having at his disposal millions of soldiers, an undefeated fleet, and abundant transports, within a few hours' steaming of our coast, no Government dare rely, or would be allowed to do so by public opinion, solely upon the Navy for the security of England, the nerve-centre of the whole Empire." [1]

Granted. But then the public opinion, to which the Government defers, should be a well-instructed public opinion. The Germans, it seems, were well instructed ; for they attempted no invasion, not even a raid except of the tip-and-run kind. For raids by landing they substituted air raids ; and they concentrated on what is England's weak point, her imported food.

[1] Sir W. Robertson, " From Private to Field-Marshal," p. 192.

# IV

# THE STRUGGLE FOR THE MEDITERRANEAN
## IN THE EIGHTEENTH CENTURY [1]

ONE of the chief lessons of the wars waged by
William III. against Louis XIV. was the potency of
naval operations against the French Mediterranean seaboard.  As Richelieu had made of Toulon a great dockyard
and arsenal whence a French fleet could threaten both Spain
and the medley of Italian states, so William was resolved,
not only to end that coercion, but also to retort the naval
argument on France herself. She, whose first Mediterranean
admiral, the Duc de Brézé, had cast a medal bearing the
legend "Présage de l'Empire de la Mer", was soon to
experience on her southern coasts the pressure of Anglo-
Dutch fleets, which helped to bring about the unstable
compromise known as the Peace of Ryswick (1697).

Yet, before the death of William III. in 1702, the
Mediterranean seemed again to be about to become a
French lake.  For Philip V., grandson of Louis XIV.,
was King of Spain, while the Hapsburg claimant, styled
"Charles III.," received support from the former Allies,
but none from the Spaniards.  A Franco-Spanish world-
dominion appearing imminent, the Allies bound themselves
by treaty to prevent the union of those two crowns, and to
ensure to "Charles III." the possession of the then Spanish
Netherlands, the Milanese, and Naples.  The English Parliament declared French domination of the Mediterranean
to be fatal to the repose of the world ; and Britons, Dutch

[1] Paper read at the Brussels Historical Congress of 1923.

and the subjects of the Emperor resolved to re-establish the balance of power both on land and sea.

During the ensuing War of the Spanish Succession the brilliant exploits of Marlborough and Prince Eugene obscured somewhat the achievements of the Admirals, Rooke, Clowdisley Shovell, and Leake.   Yet these sailors, and those of Holland, contributed largely to the final issue.   In 1703–1704 the operations of the Anglo-Dutch fleet off the coasts of Spain induced her to spread out her forces, with the result that Gibraltar was left with a mere handful of troops —80 regulars and 396 volunteers.   An attack by the Anglo-Dutch fleet (16 British, 6 Dutch), and the assault of a landing force of marines from the side of the isthmus soon overpowered the brave but inadequate garrison (July 21, 1704).   With the loss of only 61 killed and 252 wounded the Allies secured the key of the Mediterranean.

The prize was not to go uncontested.   A French fleet of 51 sail, under the Count of Toulouse, received orders from Madrid to recover the stronghold.   With the same end in view Franco-Spanish forces marched southwards to besiege it from the isthmus.   On August 24 Toulouse and Rooke met off Malaga, 50 French ships *versus* 51 rather smaller units of the Allies.   Tactically, the battle was indecisive : for not a ship was taken, burnt, or sunk on either side. Strategically, the balance was in favour of the Allies.   The whole of the next day they lay-to to the leeward, challenging the *fleur de lys* to renew the fight.   Toulouse did not close; and, on the following morning, when the English and Dutch ships bore towards him, he sheered off northwards.   They stood-away westwards for Gibraltar ; and for that reason Toulouse claimed the victory.   Never was claim more hollow.   Toulouse had set out to retake Gibraltar ; whereas it was the Allies who now put in and strengthened the garrison.   He retired to Toulon and laid up his ships.   The Allies held the Straits.   If, therefore, we judge of this battle by its results, it must count as a triumph for the Allies.   Thereafter, despite three desperate efforts of the Bourbon fleets to retake the fortress, it remained intact.

The full import of that conquest did not appear at once. What was apparent was the immensity of the military efforts put forth by French and Spaniards to recover the post, and the comparative ease by which they were beaten off by a small garrison and the covering fleet of Admiral Leake. North of the isthmus France and Spain assembled forces which might have turned the scale on other fronts. Indeed, in nearly every war down to 1801, a large part of the best Spanish troops was " contained " by the impregnable Rock.

But even more important, though less obvious, were the naval results. Now the Allies divided the navies of the Bourbon Powers. They cut off the Toulon and Cartagena fleets from those at Cadiz, Ferrol, Brest, and Rochefort. Thenceforth the first move of France and Spain, at least in any major operation, was an attempt to reunite those severed portions. Until their Atlantic and Mediterranean forces effected a junction, nothing great—say an invasion of England on a great scale [1]—could be essayed. By occupying Gibraltar the Allies acquired a commanding central position, such as, in the hands of an active and enterprising enemy, influences the fortunes, not only of a campaign, but of the whole war. We may go further and say that the capture of Gibraltar decided the main outlines of Mediterranean campaigns ; for it neutralised to a large extent the value of Toulon in world-warfare. That naval base had been developed by Richelieu and Louis XIV. as a means of overawing the neighbouring peninsulas. After 1704 the Toulon fleet was isolated, and about one-third of the naval resources of France was cut off from the major portion, so long as the British fleet held the Gibraltar defile.

For France the War of the Spanish Succession now became almost entirely *une guerre de course*, whose details

---

[1] Of course smaller efforts at invasion were made, as in 1708 by Forbin from Dunkirk to the Firth of Forth. (See Terry on " The Jacobite Movements of 1701–1720 " ; and P. Coquelle on " Invasion Schemes " in " *Rev. d'Histoire diplomatique*," 1901.)

cover only ten pages in the work of Capitaine Troude,
" Batailles navales de la France." We here cannot so
lightly dismiss the years 1705–12. They are marked by
two important episodes, the attempt against Toulon in 1707,
and the capture of Minorca in 1708. The dash at Toulon
was an attempt which had been strongly advised, first by
William III., then by Marlborough, to cripple France in
the south both by land and sea. It offered just that
example of potent diversion whereby French military
pressure could be lessened alike on Flanders, Spain, and
Italy. In 1707 the need of such a stroke was pressing.
An Allied army crossed the Maritime Alps, and, helped by
the fleet of Sir Clowdisley Shovell, advanced on Toulon,
which was to be blockaded also by sea. The enterprise
so nearly succeeded that the French sank most of their fleet
in the Inner Road, thus seriously crippling their naval
and military efforts.[1]

Still more decisive was the conjoint expedition against
the stronghold of Port Mahon in Minorca. The Anglo-
Dutch fleet, under Admiral Leake, brought up a considerable landing force under General Stanhope; and by
effective co-operation they soon reduced that fortress.
This event realised the hopes and demands of the Allied
leaders. "Charles III.," Marlborough, and the Dutch
Estates had agreed that victory would not be theirs until
a great Allied fleet could be maintained all the year round
in the Mediterranean ; for only so could Toulon be kept
continuously sealed, and the coasts of Catalonia and Italy
safe from insult. Port Mahon, being 250 miles to windward
of Toulon and half that distance from Barcelona, fulfilled
all the conditions of a central position and a large and easily
defensible harbour. Those advantages had been discerned
by William III., who had actually bargained with Louis
for Minorca during the parleys of 1701. Now the Allies
gained it in fair fight. Stanhope, who commanded the

---

[1] Villars, who with a French army had invaded Baden, was ordered
to retreat and send off troops to Provence. (Lavisse, " Hist. de France,"
viii. 108.)

landing force, took care to leave there only British troops, and at the peace the island remained British. Its retention has been strongly condemned by Señor Duro and other writers ; for Minorca surrendered to " Charles III.," not to England. Seeing, however, that of late the Dutch fleet had been almost inactive, that by 1713 the cause of Charles fell to the ground, and that Spain now remained under Philip V. (*i.e.* closely connected with France) it would have been surprising if the nation whose fleet had almost entirely achieved both the capture and the preservation of Gibraltar and Minorca had handed back those prizes to a virtually hostile power.[1]

It is clear, then, that naval as well as military events contributed to the restoration of the balance of power effected by the Treaty of Utrecht (1713). That equipoise, resting on a Mediterranean basis, was soon threatened by the ambitious schemes of Cardinal Alberoni on behalf of Spain ; but these were frustrated in 1718 by the destruction of the Spanish fleet off Cape Passaro, also by the temporary alliance of France and Great Britain. Thereafter the two Bourbon courts came to accord by the Family Compacts of 1733 and 1743, the chief aims being to set limits to British expansion beyond the seas and to overthrow Hapsburg ascendancy in the Belgic Netherlands and Italy. The confused and shifting strifes known as the War of the Austrian Succession need not be traced here ; but we may note that sea power played its part on the following occasions :

(1) A British squadron despatched to Naples compelled that court to return to neutrality and withdraw its contingent from the Bourbon forces campaigning in the Romagna (August 1742).

(2) Admiral Matthews' sea fight off Toulon in February 1744 (albeit indecisive owing to the shameful slackness of his second-in-command, Lestock) frustrated the intentions of the great Franco-Spanish fleet, and maintained for the

[1] Whitaker's squadron, which remained behind till Port Mahon surrendered, comprised 18 British and 3 Dutch ships. (Corbett, p. 522.)

present a general Anglo-Austrian ascendancy in those waters.

(3) In 1745, however, the British Mediterranean fleet was mostly withdrawn owing to the threatening situation in Great Britain.

(4) Consequently the French army about to invade Italy was able to advance almost unhindered along the Corniche Road to Savona (a road which is nearly everywhere open to the fire of ships' guns) and thence to invade Piedmont by the easy pass which, half a century later, Bonaparte was to render famous.

(5) In 1746, when the British could again despatch a large fleet to the Mediterranean, it severed the communications of the French invaders. Co-operating with an Austrian army, the ships harassed the French along that same narrow seaboard, almost cutting off their retreat near Mentone, and helping on an Austrian incursion into the county of Nice.[1]

Thereupon the British Mediterranean fleet was ineffectively handled by Admirals Medley and Byng; but naval pressure on the French coasts and commerce was so far cogent that the war ended in a stalemate. The Peace of Aix-la-Chapelle (1748) restored the *status quo ante bellum.* Thus sea power, exerted largely in the Mediterranean, had nullified the effects of the brilliant victories of the Maréchal de Saxe in the Netherlands.

We may pass rapidly over the Seven Years' War and the War of American Independence; for, so far as Great Britain was concerned, they were almost entirely colonial. It is significant, however, that, in April 1756, France opened hostilities in Europe by a sudden attack on Minorca, which, owing to the incredible slackness of Admiral Byng, completely succeeded. The loss of Port Mahon, the citadel of which by this time was very strong, caused a profound sensation—so much so that, in the following December, England's only ally, Frederic the Great, secretly advised her to seize Corsica as a set-off to Minorca. The suggestion

[1] Richmond, " The Navy in the War of 1739–48," vol. iii. 155, 162.

shows his sense of the potential value of British naval pressure in the Mediterranean.[1]

After capturing Minorca France was comparatively safe from all interference on that side, and could therefore prepare to use her Toulon fleet in the traditional way for the great game in the Atlantic or in the Channel. Thus, both on diplomatic and strategic grounds, her capture of Minorca seems to have been the best possible gambit. On this question I dissent, though with diffidence, from an acknowledged authority on naval history, whose untimely death we deeply deplore—I mean Sir Julian Corbett. In his work " England in the Seven Years' War," ch. v., he states that the French effort against Minorca involved a strategical error, because Minorca had no relation to the object of the war. That criticism is conclusive as regards the cause and ultimate issues of the war. But it is not conclusive as regards war methods. Experience had taught British leaders the effectiveness of pressure applied to the southern coasts of France ; and she sought to avert such pressure by the capture of the base whence it could be most vigorously exerted. She also hoped to win over Spain by means of the bait of Minorca, and then, as mistress of the Mediterranean, prepare for a heavy blow against Great Britain or the British colonies.

Despite the annoying neutrality of the court of Madrid, France sought to unite her Toulon fleet with her Biscay fleet for such an offensive. The efforts failed both in 1758 and 1759 owing to the vigilance of the British commanders operating from Gibraltar as base. To notice only the latter case : in August 1759 the Toulon fleet of 12 sail, under de La Clue, almost succeeded in eluding the British watch-dogs under Boscawen, and hoped to slip away northwards and entrap the British blockaders off Brest. But, against such an admiral as Boscawen, incomplete success involved ultimate failure. The running fight which ended in mid-August at Lagos virtually destroyed the Toulon fleet.

[1] France then had as allies Austria and Russia, but not Spain (at least openly) until January 1762.

Thus, thanks to Boscawen's watchfulness in the Straits, the French did not get away from the Mediterranean and did not overpower the British blockaders off Brest. Never was the value of Gibraltar proved more decisively ; and the importance assigned to Minorca appeared in the resolve of Pitt to capture Belleisle in order to exchange it for Minorca at the peace, as indeed came about in 1763.

During the American War of Independence the British navy was outmatched so soon as France openly supported the United States (March 1778). As it could not prevent the Toulon fleet from entering the ocean, or blockade that of Brest, the chief naval battles were fought off the coasts of North America. And after Spain declared war in June 1779, Great Britain would, I think, have acted wisely in evacuating Minorca, and withdrawing from the Mediterranean in order the better to concentrate on the defence of Gibraltar. Minorca was chiefly of value as a base for watching Toulon. When it was impossible to maintain a British fleet in that sea, the island was of little worth ; and the attempt to defend it involved a dangerous diffusion of naval and military strength. Its garrison could not be relieved ; and after a brave defence General Murray had to surrender Port Mahon with his garrison of about 2500 men (February 5, 1782).

Very different was the case of Gibraltar. That position was invaluable, even in those defensive campaigns ; but the Rock could be relieved only thrice during a siege of three and a half years (June 1779–February 1783). General Eliott and his brave garrison repelled the determined efforts of the Bourbon Powers. Consequently Great Britain, though isolated and overborne, was able to end the war without discredit, and (if we except Minorca) with few serious losses outside North America. Spain pressed hard for the cession of Gibraltar. But Eliott's glorious feat had made its retention a point of honour on which the nation, even in its dire straits, would not give way.[1] Therefore, though deprived

[1] George III. and some Ministers would at first have ceded it for a sufficient indemnity. (Fitzmaurice, " Life of Shelburne," iii. 305 ; Rose, " Life of Pitt," i. 114.)

of the greater part of her colonial empire, Great Britain was not wholly driven from the Mediterranean; and she therefore retained one of the essentials of maritime greatness.

Her position was far more favourable in February 1793, when the French Republic declared war on her and Holland. She then joined a great coalition, framed in 1792 by Austria, Prussia, and Sardinia, to which were added in 1793 the Empire, Spain, and Naples. The experience of former wars having demonstrated the necessity of defending our Mediterranean Allies by the despatch of a powerful fleet to that sea, Spain, Naples, and Sardinia demanded that an adequate force be sent in order to protect them from the Toulon fleet, then being strengthened for some aggressive move. Largely owing to these political reasons, the Admiralty despatched to the Mediterranean the first British fleet that was ready for sea, even though, in the then acute lack of seamen, that step involved leaving the Brest fleet unwatched until the middle of July. The arrival of the British fleet under Lord Hood off Toulon had the effect of knitting together a hitherto loose Mediterranean league. There followed a singular and wholly unexpected series of events which opened up even more brilliant prospects. The Toulon Royalists, fearing savage reprisals by the Jacobins, decided to entrust their town and fleet to the British and Spanish fleets then in the vicinity (August 28-29). This great opportunity, surpassing the wildest dreams of William III. and Marlborough, was, however, frittered away owing to the strange mistakes and unworthy jealousies of the Allies; and the defence collapsed on December 18.

Thereafter Spain became half-hearted in the common cause; and when Hood sought to occupy Corsica as a base for the observation of Toulon her jealousies increased. In the sequel Paoli and the Corsican Royalists, who invited Hood there, proved to be utterly intractable; in the autumn of 1796 British officers in general rejoiced at the decision to evacuate the island.[1] Politically, it was

[1] "Spencer Papers," ii. 74; Nicolas, "Letters of Nelson," ii. 69, 213, 298.

untenable.   Strategically, it had been of considerable value
as a base whence the French efforts at invading the
Genoese Riviera could be thwarted.   But, by a curious
fatality, the command of the British Mediterranean fleet
early in 1795 devolved upon Admiral Hotham, who, after
letting slip two good opportunities of inflicting decisive
defeats on the reorganized Toulon fleet, could devote little
attention to the support of our Austrian and Sardinian
allies then facing the French army near Loano.

These difficult duties fell to the lot of Hotham's ablest
subordinate, Nelson, whose letters teem with complaints
as to the paucity of his light cruisers and the need of greater
energy in harassing the French advance along the Corniche.
He also asserted that while his squadron held Vado Bay
Italy was safe.[1]   But that same truth having been grasped
by Carnot, Bonaparte, and Masséna, they strained every
nerve to capture Vado and Savona.   The secession of
Spain from the First Coalition in July 1795 enabled them
to strengthen the French, who after receiving supplies
by sea attacked and utterly routed the Austro-Sardinian
forces at Loano (November 23, 1795).[2]   Nelson strove hard
to repair this disaster ; [3] but it was irreparable.   Vado Bay
and Savona were lost.   In April 1796 Bonaparte carried
the war into the interior of Piedmont, severed the allied
armies, and compelled Sardinia to a peace.   The sequel
was the conquest of North and Central Italy ; and that feat
was accomplished with equal brilliance and soundness of
judgment, so that no retort attempted either by Austria's
whitecoats or by British bluejackets had any appreciable
effect.   The parallel with 1745 breaks down so soon as
Bonaparte left the Riviera and severed the allied armies.
The land power seemed now about to reverse the verdict
of 1704–08 in the Mediterranean.

There followed in October 1796 the declaration of war
by Spain on Great Britain.   Threatened nearer home by

[1] Nicolas, ii. 129, 136.
[2] Jomini, " Guerres de la Rév.," vii. p. 308, emphasises the importance
to Masséna of the arrival of stores by sea.          [3] Nicolas, ii. 151.

the French conquest of Holland and by revolts in Ireland, the British Government decided to abandon the Mediterranean and to concentrate its fleets off Lisbon, in the Channel, and the North Sea. This decision led to momentous results. It hastened the collapse of the Austrian defence in North Italy ; but the concentration of British naval strength in the Atlantic and in home waters enabled Jervis and Duncan respectively to deal sharp blows to the Spanish and Dutch navies at St. Vincent and Camperdown. Meanwhile, French domination of the Mediterranean (now seemingly complete) led to the formation of world-shaking designs. Bonaparte was laying his plans for securing the Ionian Isles, Malta, and the Venetian fleet, with a view to the seizure of Egypt as a prelude to the conquest of India. So threatening were his moves, even in Europe, that, early in 1798, Austria prepared to renew the war provided that Great Britain despatched a powerful fleet into the Mediterranean—a demand founded on the efficacy of sea power in that area, as was proven in 1704–12, 1718, 1742, 1746, and 1793. Despite the apprehensions felt by the British Admiralty at so daring a step, while the British Isles were threatened with invasion, Pitt and Grenville insisted that a fleet must be sent to the Mediterranean. It was despatched in April 1798, primarily in order to defend Naples and Sicily from the great Armada preparing at Toulon, and to assist Austria to eject the French from Italy. The real objective of Bonaparte's Armada, viz. Egypt, was as yet unsuspected, and it remained a mystery until Captain Hood of the " Zealous " sighted the masts of the French fleet in Aboukir Bay on the afternoon of August 1, 1798.

Then, and only then, was surmised the marvellous orientation of world-politics effected by Bonaparte. For the first time since the Crusades a strong eastern trend was imparted to European policy ; and the eastern half of the Mediterranean forthwith acquired an importance equal to the western half. Egypt, Malta, and Corfu became the storm centres of the diplomatic world, which thenceforth had far more to think about than its previous preoccupation, the balance of power in the West Mediterranean.

For a time Nelson's aquiline swoop on the fleet of Admiral Brueys ended the grandiose schemes of Bonaparte and shut off his army in Egypt. French domination of the Mediterranean, which of late had seemed assured, vanished during the night of August 1. Minorca speedily fell to the Union Jack, and the Ionian Isles to a Russo-Turkish force. The entry into the West Mediterranean of Admiral Bruix with a great Franco-Spanish fleet in May 1799 with the aim of reversing the verdict of the Nile ended with a tame retreat to the Atlantic; and the surrender of the French garrison of Valetta sixteen months later terminated, for the present, Bonaparte's schemes for the domination of the Mediterranean—*but principal de ma politique*. The end of the century saw Bonaparte, after his escape to France, triumphant on land, but the " Army of Egypt " still cut off and the Ionian Isles in the possession of a Russo-Turkish force. Thus a century of convulsive efforts concluded with a distribution of power in the Mediterranean between all the nations having important interests in that sea.

The settlement reached at the Peace of Amiens (March 1802) everywhere lacked finality. Spain received Minorca, Malta was handed back to the moribund Order of the Knights of St. John, the Ionian Isles became a republic which France and Russia equally coveted, and Egypt was subjected to the weak and exasperating rule of the Turks. Thus the sea power, which once again had been the backbone of a great coalition for the purpose of restoring equilibrium in Europe, left Mediterranean affairs in a state of flux and confusion comparable to that of the year 1702. The renewal of the war in May 1803 arose mainly out of this confusion and the manifest resolve of Napoleon to renew his oriental designs.

The evidence passed under review seems to warrant the following conclusions :

(1) The chief problem of Mediterranean politics during

nearly the whole of the eighteenth century lay in the
confusion and weakness, first of the Spanish realm, and
thereafter of the Italian states.   Aggressive designs on
those peninsulas were checked most effectively by the
intervention of the Allied fleets, which up to the year 1796
frustrated the plans of the invaders.   Sea-control, exercised
in the West Mediterranean, was the chief steadying
influence in the politics of Western and Southern Europe.
But in 1796 that control was defied by Bonaparte with
startling success, for the reasons suggested above.

(2) The general course of Mediterranean politics in the
eighteenth century tends to show that that sea is essentially
an international area which can belong to no one Power, or
even to a combination of riparian Powers.   It is an international area because free access to its waters is necessary
not only to the dwellers on or near the shores, but also
to all nations having important commercial dealings with
them.   Any attempt, therefore, to impose local control
was resisted by nearly the whole of Europe, as happened
in 1702 against Louis XIV., in 1718 against Alberoni, in
1746 against Louis XV., in 1798 against Bonaparte.

(3) There has been a strong tendency to establish a
balance of Mediterranean power among the nations having
weighty interests in those waters.   All efforts to upset that
balance, as in the years cited above, immediately provoked
counterstrokes which aimed at restoring the political
equipoise in that sea.

(4) In 1798 Bonaparte's Egyptian expedition diverted
attention to Malta, the Ionian Isles, and the Levant.
Thenceforth the Eastern Mediterranean rivalled in importance the Western Mediterranean.   The two halves of
that sea became a political unit, and the whole expanse
came to be regarded, not only as an area for influencing
the fortunes of the west, but also as a channel for reaching
the east.   The international character of the Mediterranean
Sea thereby attained a new and enhanced significance,
which was soon to be affirmed by the joint efforts for the
suppression of the Barbary pirates.

# V

# THE INFLUENCE OF SEA POWER ON INDIAN HISTORY (1746–1802) [1]

IT is a singular fact that India, with its vast extent of sea coast, should not have been powerfully affected by great maritime peoples until late in its history. This statement does not leave out of count the influence exerted by the Arabs, Portuguese, and Dutch, which for a time was considerable along the Malabar and Coromandel coasts. But by degrees, and for causes which we cannot here discuss, it declined ; and unquestionably the forces which moulded the fortunes of the Indian peoples set in chiefly from the passes of the North West. From the time of the Aryan inroads to that of the incursion of Nadir Shah in 1739 and Ahmad Shah in 1756, the fate of India depended mainly on her ability, or inability, to resist the pressure of the warlike tribes of Central Asia, Afghanistan, and Baluchistan.

The influence of sea power on the fate of the Peninsula became paramount towards the middle of the eighteenth century. At that time the ravages of Nadir Shah and the increasing weakness of the Mogul dynasty brought the land to a state of anarchy. Such a condition of things favoured the intervention of new political forces, and they came from a quarter where no one of the Indian princes could challenge them, viz. from the sea. During sixty years the keen rivalry of Great Britain and France in Europe led to contests for the sovereignty of the seas and the possession of the lands watered by the Ganges and the

---

[1] Reprinted from the "Indian Historical Journal" (1924).

Kistna, by the St. Lawrence and the Ohio.  As is well known, the eager imaginations of the French proconsuls, Dumas and Dupleix in India, Lasalle and La Galissonnière in Canada, first traced out schemes of wide dominion which they sought to attain by means of alliances with native chieftains and by the use of native troops.  At first both in India and in Canada their skill, enterprise, and superior organisation won notable successes over the more lethargic Briton.  To the superficial eye their triumph seemed assured.  In reality the last word lay with sea power ; for successes in the Carnatic and on the Canadian border lands were useless if supplies from Europe were cut off. The French admiral La Bourdonnais (for the time supreme off the Coromandel coast) might capture Madras, as he did in September 1746, but of what avail was this conquest if he and Dupleix entered into long and bitter disputes as to the disposal of the place—disputes which lasted until, in mid-October, the monsoon burst upon the French fleet, destroyed half of it, and crippled the remainder ?  The episode illustrated the evil results of discord between the authorities on sea and land : but the lesson was lost on the French Government, which subsequently sent out the choleric General Lally, whose violent temper wrecked all chance of cordial co-operation between the two services. Great Britain throughout was far more fortunate in securing harmony between them.

Furthermore, in 1746–48, France herself was undergoing slow but sure exhaustion by the exploits of the fleets of Anson and Hawke.  The fate of Madras, therefore, depended finally on hostilities proceeding in the Bay of Biscay and in the English Channel.  There, French squadrons and French commerce were swept from the seas : and early in 1748 the *Ministre des Finances* declared that he saw Hell's mouth opening before him if the war continued another year.  But how restore French seaborne commerce, when the French navy was reduced to 22 sail-of-the-line ? [1]

[1] Chevalier, " La Marine française," vol. i. p. 49,

Such were the fundamental facts in the spring of 1748, which induced Louis XV. to make peace on condition that conquests were to be restored by both sides. Madras therefore reverted to the East India Company. Probably that event would have occurred finally if the war had continued ; for in July 1748 the British Admiral Boscawen arrived off Cuddalore (Fort St. David) and mustered in all 10 sail-of-the-line and transports, having on board 3200 troops. But storms and rains thwarted his operations against Pondichery, and the campaign on land ended in favour of the French, when news of the peace arrived. Accordingly the restoration of Madras to the British aroused surprise and eager comment in every court and bazaar in India. Usually, peace returned to her plains only when whole districts had been ravaged and myriads had been slaughtered. Now Fort St. George once again flew the flag of its patron saint, and the whole Carnatic had rest, owing to some mysterious agency which reversed all the visible operations of war.

Here was the first outstanding illustration of a highly important fact, that thenceforth the fortunes of India were often to be controlled by events occurring far away on an element which most of her teeming millions never saw, and never thought of without wonder and dread. But similar events soon occurred. Dupleix was not the man quietly to renounce his roseate hopes. Therefore, as soon as Boscawen set sail for Europe, the French took the field and assailed Tanjore. The unofficial warfare which ensued is too complex and indecisive to call for treatment here : and we can only note that in 1754 the rival Companies came to an amicable settlement on the general basis of non-interference in the affairs of the Native States.[1] The exponents of a "forward policy," viz. Dupleix, Clive, and Stringer Lawrence were also recàlled.

Nevertheless the renewal of hostilities by the French on the river Ohio in that very year rekindled a conflagration

---

[1] Colonel Lawrence, "Narrative of the War on the Coast of Coromandel," pp. 5, 95-100.

both in Europe and in India. Their forward moves from Canada to the Mississippi fatally compromised their fortunes in India : for that essential factor, the French navy, was unequal to the strain of war in North America, Europe, and India. During the peace it had been comparatively neglected, so that in 1756 it numbered only about 50 efficient sail-of-the-line [1] as against nearly 100 British. Spain, the natural ally of France, would not help her until early in 1762. Therefore, apart from the first dash, at Minorca, her navy remained almost uniformly on the defensive—an attitude which involved ultimate failure in all the overseas campaigns. Owing to the extravagance and ineptitude of the Pompadour régime, France had not the funds for maintaining three separate wars, those in Europe, Canada, and India. Moreover, Pitt's masterly concentration on the essential points assured her failure at all points.

India occupied only the third place in the counsels of Versailles. As Canada took precedence, the chief French expedition to the Carnatic was long delayed. Not until May 1757 did Commodore d'Aché set sail with the main body from Brest, with a small force of warships and transports, conveying two regiments of infantry. Driven back by mishaps due to weather and inexperience, he then had three of his sail-of-the-line taken away to be sent to Canada. The spring of the year 1758 was ending before he sighted the Coromandel coast. General Lally, the new Governor-General of the French East Indies, was on board. His instructions bade him withdraw from the engagements formally contracted by the Company with the native princes " which, like the war, are equally ruinous and prejudicial to commerce " : and he was ordered to limit his efforts to the capture of places on the coast.[2] Thus, France intended to restrict her responsibilities in the East, waging there a limited war, while throwing her strength into the European and Canadian campaigns.

---

[1] Lavisse, " Hist. de France," vol. viii. p. 272.
[2] Lacour-Gayet, " La Marine militaire sous Louis XV," ch. 22 ; Waddington, " Guerre de Sept. Ans," iii. pp. 380-383.

It was, however, too late thus to circumscribe her efforts. Her agents in India, especially General de Bussy at Hyderabad, had challenged England to a duel *à outrance* : and reliance on them had in part induced Siraj-ud-daula to attack and capture Calcutta (June 20, 1756). The ensuing events are too well known to call for narration. What concerns us is the resolve of the British authorities at Madras in July to despatch Colonel Clive with all the troops then available on board the squadron of Admiral Watson for the recovery of Calcutta. Never has a council of merchants framed a more daring plan : for it involved the withdrawal both of the squadron and of the little army on which depended the safety of Fort St. George even when the outbreak of war in Europe was known to be imminent. Indeed, if the Brest dockyard men had worked more efficiently, d'Aché's force would have reached Madras long before the British succours. In that case Clive must have been recalled from Bengal long before his work was completed. It should be remembered that only the skill and tenacity of Lawrence in the Carnatic, seconded by command of the sea, enabled the British to hold out in that quarter against greatly superior forces, while Clive and Watson struck hard in Bengal.

The despatch of Watson and Clive was decisive in one other respect. The co-operation of fleet and army in the river Hughli offered as brilliant an example of a conjoint expedition as that of Admiral Saunders and General Wolfe two years later in the river St. Lawrence, and in each case the expedition was sent at a favourable time and up a river which led easily into the heart of the continent. Watson's squadron consisted of 5 men-of-war and 5 transports, having on board about 900 European troops and 1500 sepoys. Weighing anchor from Madras roads on October 16, 1756, it soon met with the northerly gales heralding the monsoon, and had to stand over to the coast of Aracan before it could beat up to the mouth of the Hughli. There, in December, after rescuing the refugees from Calcutta, it began to work up the difficult channels towards that city.

Captain Speke of H.M.S. " Kent " distinguished himself by his skill in guiding the fleet up the river, thus covering Clive's right flank and contributing materially to the capture of the outlying forts and posts. Late on January 1, 1757, Watson sent the boats of the squadron upstream to burn some fireships which the enemy had prepared below Fort William. The enterprise was successful ; and on the morrow the "Kent," "Tiger," and two smaller craft worked up towards Fort William, Clive marching his troops on a parallel course. At 10.20 A.M. the ships opened fire on the fort, and, with the help of the troops, drove out the Nawab's forces by midday. The British lost 9 seamen and 3 soldiers killed, and 26 seamen and 5 soldiers wounded. It is clear that the ships' guns played the chief part in the recovery of Fort William. Thereupon a detachment of seamen assisted Clive in land operations which induced Siraj-ud-daula to sue for peace, which was signed on February 7.

That treaty was illusory ; for the Nawab was found to be intriguing for the armed help of the French, especially that of General de Bussy, whose position in the Circars was formidable.[1] We may pause to notice that Siraj-ud-daula, somewhat like Tippoo Sahib forty years later, framed his final aggressive resolve in utter disregard of the factor of sea power. He relied on de Bussy's control of man-power in the Deccan and the Circars, but took little or no thought of the element of surprise which command of the ocean so often confers. The advance of the British fleet up the Hughli had confounded his schemes ; but, seemingly, he believed that that fleet could effect little more. He was wrong, for now there arrived three more ships, with troops on board ; and, later on, he was to experience the stinging power of a flotilla high up the river.

Watson now strongly urged Clive to settle matters with the French in Bengal before they could draw on de Bussy's reserves of force only some 300 miles away. His advice,

---

[1] Owen Cambridge, " Transactions on the Coast of Coromandel," pp. 135-137.

concurring with that contained in the Company's despatches lately received from London, induced Clive to commit his Madras troops still further ; and the squadron and little army moved on the French capital at Chandernagore. This contained a citadel fronting the Hughli and mounting some 60 guns. Four batteries further south barred the landward and river approaches from that side ; but the garrison of 145 European troops and 300 sepoys, besides 300 volunteers, was unequal to the emergency. On March 16 Clive, by a skilful move from the north-west, compelled the evacuation of all the batteries save the one commanding the river. Here Captain Speke was pushing on a reconnaissance by boats, the soundings of which, corroborated by news brought by a deserter, showed that the vessels recently sunk by the French did not block the fairway. Slowly then, but surely, the " Kent " (70), " Tiger " (60), " Salisbury " (50), and small craft beat up towards Chandernagore. By the 23rd all was ready for a combined attack. The " Kent " suffered severely from the fire of the citadel ; drifting downstream she was badly raked, and prevented the " Salisbury " from getting into an effective position. The honours of the day therefore rested with the " Tiger," whose salvoes wrought destruction within the citadel. The French with their usual gallantry " stood to their guns as long as they had any to fire "—so writes the surgeon of the " Kent." But the double attack was overpowering, and after three hours' conflict the brave de Vigne surrendered Chandernagore. The ships had lost 33 killed and 128 wounded. Clive's troops lost only 1 killed and 10 wounded.[1]

The brilliance of Clive's victory at Plassey has somewhat obscured the success at Chandernagore ; but the latter was of the first importance as providing a sure basis for that dramatic exploit. So soon as Siraj-ud-daula showed clear signs of hostility, Clive marched northwards, with his flank protected by a huge flotilla. Thanks to it, he captured Katwa fort with ease, and then near Plassey awaited the

[1] Orme, ii. pp. 137-142 ; Malleson, " The French in India," ch. xi. ; Clowes, " The Royal Navy," iii. 160-163.

outcome of his secret bargainings with Mir Jafar. As is well known, Clive and a majority of the officers at first opposed an attack on the Nawab's immense array. Finally, thanks to the counsels of Eyre Coote, he resolved to attack ; but it is reasonable to suppose that the presence of his flotilla supplied, not only the means of crossing the river for the assault, but also a moral and material support which prompted his ultimate resolve.

Rightly considered, then, the Plassey campaign is an example of a conjoint operation of fleet and army conducted under advantageous conditions. All students of war admit that, without the fleet and flotilla of Admiral Saunders, General Wolfe could not have taken Quebec in 1759. But it is equally demonstrable that Watson and his captains contributed very materially towards the recovery of Calcutta and the capture of Chandernagore ; while the fleet's proboscis, the flotilla, played an essential part in the brilliant finale at Plassey.[1]  Indeed, the whole campaign would have been criminally rash had not Watson's fleet provided both formidable powers of attack and a means of retreat if necessary.

Unfortunately Admiral Watson died on August 16, 1757, when the fruits of victory were being reaped. But his successor, Rear-Admiral Pocock, was able to meet the heavy responsibilities awaiting him off the Coromandel Coast. Returning thither with ships badly in need of repair, he, on April 29, 1758, administered a severe check to d'Aché's somewhat superior force, which had at last arrived from France. Misconduct by certain captains on both sides rendered the action indecisive, but while the French suffered more in men, the British suffered so much aloft as to be unable to effect the relief of Fort St. David (Cuddalore), which surrendered to the French on June 2. Thus the arrival of d'Aché accelerated the capture of the second most important of the British Coromandel posts.

Thereafter the advantage lay with Pocock. For on

[1] It is singular that Mahan (" Influence of Sea Power on History," pp. 292, 305) scarcely refers to the influence of Watson's squadron in deciding the campaign in Bengal.

August 3 he handled the French so roughly that their Commodore, in spite of the vehement remonstrances of Lally, resolved to bear away for the dockyard at l'Île de France. Pocock made for Bombay. The sequel proved the vital importance of having a good naval base near at hand. At Bombay dockyard, though it was still in a rudimentary stage, Pocock found means to repair and replenish his ships, and was back off the Coromandel coast by April 7, 1759. But at l'Île de France everything had gone to ruin since the recall of La Bourdonnais, and the loss of Chandernagore deprived that island of its chief source of food supply. The lack of stores and provisions put d'Aché to such shifts that he did not reach Pondichery until August 15.

Meanwhile, the loss of control of the sea told severely on the French operations in the Carnatic. Lally, though long hampered by want of money and transport, began the siege of Madras in mid-December 1758, with a force comprising 3200 Europeans, about 4000 Sepoys, 20 heavy siege guns, and 10 mortars. Inside Fort St. George, Lawrence had only 1800 Europeans, and between two and three thousand Sepoys. The fort was ill protected towards the sea, and the arrival of d'Aché would fatally have compromised the defence. But at the crisis the Union flag, not the *fleur de lys*, came on the scene. At the end of January 1759, when Lally hoped soon to master the place, a British ship appeared, threw in supplies, and brought to Lawrence news of approaching succour from the sea. It arrived on February 16. Captain Kempenfelt then hove to off the fort, with two 20-gun ships and 6 store vessels, and landed reinforcements and supplies. Never has so small a naval force effected so great a result : for, the next day, Lally hurriedly broke up his camp and retreated to Arcot, leaving behind most of his siege train.[1] This event, the beginning of the end for the French in the Carnatic, is clearly traceable to the remoteness of their naval base.

Nor was this all. For d'Aché's long absence enabled Clive to strike a decisive blow at the French and their

[1] O. Cambridge, pp. 244, 256.

partisans in the Circars.  From that long coastal region
they had fed their troops in the Carnatic, and threatened
both Clive in Bengal and the garrison of Madras.   Accordingly, he sent Colonel Forde with 500 European troops,
some 1500 sepoys, and a siege train, to help a local rajah
then in revolt against the French, and prevent the enemy
from sending further reinforcements to the aid of Lally in
the Carnatic.[1]   Forde disembarked on October 20, 1758,
near Vizagapatam, overthrew Conflans' force, and pursued
it towards Masulipatam, which he stormed by a night
attack (April 8, 1759).   These brilliant results were un-
attainable if the French fleet had been at hand to succour
those two coast towns and intercept his supplies.   As it
was, the Nizam of Hyderabad now inclined to the side of
the victors : and all the work of General de Bussy at that
Court fell to pieces like a house of cards.

The return of d'Aché's squadron of 11 ships to Pondi-
chery in mid-August promised to restore the balance in the
Carnatic.   But Pocock awaited him off Tranquebar and
there, with 8 ships, inflicted a sanguinary check on the
French superior force (September 10).   Slackness on the
part of some of d'Aché's captains spoilt his chances (for two
British ships could scarcely beat up in time for the affair).
Both sides drew off exhausted.   D'Aché declined to renew
the fight, and on September 30 again withdrew to l'Île de
France, despite the furious remonstrances of Lally.   Perhaps the admiral acted rightly in removing his battered
ships from off that exposed coast before the autumn monsoon, especially as Pocock was said to be expecting four
more sail-of-the-line from England.   In any case, his departure (this time final) dashed the last hopes of Lally
and occasioned the surrender of Pondichery by famine in
mid-January 1761.

The subsequent execution of Lally as a traitor at Paris
was a crime and a blunder : for any unprejudiced and careful investigation of his failures in the Carnatic must have
shown them to be traceable to the weakness of France at

[1] *Ibid.* pp. 244, 256 ; Dodwell, "Dupleix and Clive," pp. 176-178.

sea, to the distance of her naval base from the scene of action, and to the want of skill or determination on the part of d'Aché and some of his captains.    Lally fell a victim to mean intrigues and to ignorance regarding the efficacy of sea power.

Limits of space preclude any but the briefest survey of the war of 1778–83,[1] for indeed it led to no decisive gain in India, largely because France threw her chief weight into North America and the West Indies in order to help her American Allies.    By what proved to be a singular mis-calculation, she sent thither mediocre admirals, D'Estaing, De Guichen, and De Grasse, with fleets of great strength, while in the East Indies her ablest seaman, Suffren, com-manded a squadron only equal in size, and inferior in quality, to the British.    The naval results were therefore indecisive in both quarters.    Moreover, Suffren arrived off Pondichery a year too late to co-operate effectively with Hyder Ali, when that brilliant soldier was at the summit of his fortunes.    At that crisis the French squadron was paralysed by the indolence or cowardice of Admiral d'Orves, whose retirement from off Pondichery to l'Ile de France robbed Hyder of an otherwise certain triumph over Sir Eyre Coote.    Either by bad management or bad fortune France never had at hand an able admiral and an able general.    And now, in 1782, Suffren was badly seconded. There can be little doubt that if Suffren's captains had done their utmost, he would have destroyed Commodore John-stone's force at Porto Praja in the Cape Verde Isles.    Even with their half-hearted support he so far crippled it as to save the Cape of Good Hope from Johnstone's projected attack and thus hamper the arrival of British reinforce-ments in the East Indies.    Thereafter, Admiral Sir Edward Hughes must have succumbed in the most critical of the subsequent fights off the Coromandel coast, those of Feb-ruary 17, July 6, and September 3, 1782, but for the slack-ness or cowardice of some of the French captains.

---

[1] For details see Laughton, " Studies in Naval History," pp. 94-147 ; Malleson, " Final French Struggles in India."

The chief interest in this prolonged duel of Suffren v. Hughes lies in the singular evenness of their five determined rounds ; in the resolve of Hyder Ali (then almost supreme in the Carnatic) actively to support the French after the first round with Hughes ; and in the necessity of having naval bases near at hand for repairs. The British (now at war with the Dutch) had captured Trincomalee shortly before Suffren's arrival, and it served them well, until, after the third battle, Hughes found it necessary to refit at Madras, then an almost open roadstead. There, he was at a grave disadvantage if the French struck at Trincomalee : for the south-west monsoon was blowing and would hinder his approach from the north : while Suffren after very promptly refitting at Cuddalore (then French) had taken post at Baticaloa in the south-east of Ceylon, where he met reinforcements from France. Careful calculations showed that he would have a clear fortnight to seize Trincomalee before the British could hear of its danger and beat up against the wind to save it. He was right. He took the place with comparative ease, just two days before Hughes reappeared.[1] As to the importance of this fine natural harbour and fortified post Suffren bore testimony in a letter, June 1783, in which he declared that the very existence of the French in Indian waters depended on Trincomalee. Yet in the previous winter he had found it necessary to refit at Acheen in Sumatra and was back only just in time to save Trincomalee from Hughes who had refitted at Bombay. The campaign of 1783 ended somewhat to the advantage of the French, who with an inferior force drove off Hughes and forced him to raise the blockade of Cuddalore. Thereupon news of peace in Europe arrived.

Seeing that Great Britain was hard pressed by the French, Americans, Spaniards, and Dutch, as also by Hyder Ali, her ability to hold out with no great loss, except in the United States, was very remarkable. On the whole, the relative failure of the French may be ascribed to the dissipation of their energies, the result being that they were

[1] Colomb, " Naval Warfare," pp. 395-397.

beaten in European waters and in the West Indies.  Thanks to Rodney, Howe, and Hood, the United Kingdom defied a world of enemies and even on the Coromandel coast nearly held its own against leaders so redoubtable as Suffren and Hyder Ali.  As before in 1748, so too in 1783, the terms of peace in India depended on the general condition of the combatants, not on the situation in India herself.  Thus, because the French were suffering from commercial and financial exhaustion (the result of British sea power in home waters), the *status quo ante bellum* was virtually agreed on with Britain for their respective Indian possessions, For a similar reason, the Dutch, while recovering Trincomalee, consented to the retention of Negapatam by the British.  Most reluctantly also they conceded freedom of navigation in the hitherto closed areas of their East Indies.[1] Thus, the British gains from the Dutch (who made the mistake of protracting the negotiations until long after the other belligerents had come to terms) placed the United Kingdom in a stronger position in that quarter, and enabled it to make headway against the growing power of Tippoo Sahib.

The last struggle of the century was the most dramatic and decisive.  It arose out of the conviction of the extreme French Republicans, who leaped to power in June 1793, that Britain's power rested very largely on her control of India, which had grown more complete during the decade of peace.  This belief was shared by Bonaparte, who, after conquering Italy and partitioning the Venetian Republic with Austria, based his rapidly maturing oriental schemes on the retention of Corfu and the seizure of Malta.  Having succeeded at these two points, he thereafter easily conquered Egypt, with a view to the expulsion of the British from India.  The plan took the British and Turkish Governments by surprise ; but Nelson divined the secret ; and when his brilliant victory of the Nile (August 1, 1798) imprisoned the French in their conquest he despatched Lieutenant Duval, of H.M.S. " Zealous," to Bombay, via

[1] Koch and Schöll, " Traités," i. 456-462.

Alexandretta and Baghdad ; and the news of the blow to Bonaparte's eastern designs reached Lord Mornington, the new Governor-General, at Calcutta on October 31.[1]

Already Mornington was on the alert ; for Malartic, the French Governor of l'Île de France, had incautiously divulged the overtures privately sent to him by Tippoo Sahib. This daring chief, among his diverse schemes for the expulsion of the British, had sent two envoys to urge that governor to despatch to Mangalore a great force of 5000 Europeans and 25,000 Africans. The envoys received a warm welcome, but the governor, instead of treating the plan as one to be cautiously prepared, announced the agreement, and on January 30, 1798, asked for volunteers for the enterprise. Just 100 men came forward, and secrecy was sacrificed for this paltry result. The news reached Calcutta in June, some six weeks after " La Preneuse " frigate landed the 100 men at Mangalore. Thus, by the time Bonaparte landed in Egypt, the British authorities in India were preparing to cope with the impending crisis.

We may here pause to note the strange mistakes committed by Tippoo Sahib, Malartic, and Bonaparte. How could Tippoo have expected enough shipping to be available at l'Île de France to transport 30,000 men across the Indian Ocean ? He must surely have heard that in September 1795 the British had captured Cape Town, thus rendering extremely difficult the despatch of a large French fleet to l'Île de France. It is said that the French adventurer, Ripaud, deceived him as to the strength of the French at that point.[2] But Tippoo's credulity was certainly colossal. The imprudence of Malartic has already been noted, but it is venial by comparison with that of Bonaparte in assuming that the British, now masters of the high seas, would continue to neglect the Mediterranean and allow him to master the overland route to India. Further, how could he possibly send a great expedition to India by sea, after the events of the year 1795, when the British captured those

---

[1] James, " Naval History," ii. App. 14.
[2] Bowring, " Hyder Ali and Tipu," ch. xi.

commanding posts, Cape Town, Trincomalee, and Baticaloa ?

It is therefore difficult to take seriously his orders to
Malartic to despatch the Ile de France squadron to Suez,
still more his instructions for the building of a light squadron
at that port, where timber was scarce.  Possibly the
arrival of an Indian at Suez in December 1798, bearing a
letter which was unfortunately lost, had quickened his hopes
that the British troops were in such sore straits in India as
to justify him in taking great risks.   In reality the British
were in no great danger so long as they held the sea ; and
Nelson's prompt despatch of Duval to Bombay had shown
that it was the French who were cut off in Egypt.[1]   But the
most singular of Bonaparte's actions was his despatch from
Cairo on January 25, 1799, of a letter to Tippoo, couched
in these magniloquent terms :

" Vous avez déjà été instruit de mon arrivée sur les bords
de la mer Rouge, avec une armée innombrable et invincible,
remplie du désir de vous délivrer du joug de fer de l'Angleterre."

He then requested Tippoo to send to Suez a person with
whom to confer.[2]

In point of fact Bonaparte had with him, during his brief
excursion to Suez, a comparatively small escort ; and in
January 1799 all his plans tended towards the invasion of
Syria, which began in February.  Probably, then, his letter
to Tippoo was designed merely to urge him on to more
energetic action, so as to busy the British in that quarter,
and thus weaken them in the Mediterranean.  Whatever
were the motives underlying the letter, it probably con-
firmed the Indian in his illusions.  Mornington, after
bringing the Nizam to friendly relations and the Mahrattas
to neutrality, sought to come to an arrangement with
Tippoo, pointing out to him that the French were cut
off in Egypt.[3]  It was in vain.  Tippoo, after feigning

[1] Napoleon, " Correspondance," Nos. 3767, 3806, 3807.
[2] *Ibid.* No. 3901.
[3] Wellesley, " Correspondence," i. 59-61.

compliance, advanced his troops, and paid for his rashness with his life and his kingdom.

It is a sad story, the moral of which is the strange miscalculation of Tippoo as to the meaning of sea power and the impotence of the French to help him either from l'Île de France or Egypt. On their side the French laid their oriental plans hurriedly and without cohesion. Ripaud, the bombastic adventurer who planted the tree of liberty in Mysore, filled Tippoo with absurd hopes long before Malartic in l'Île de France or Bonaparte in Egypt could possibly satisfy a tithe of them. Between these two there was no concert ; and Malartic's precipitancy in January 1798 ruined what slight chances there were for Bonaparte to get through a few troops to Mangalore a year later. By that time Mornington had the Malabar coast patrolled by British cruisers. Moreover, on January 7, 1799, transports reached Madras with the seasoned troops promptly despatched by Lord Macartney from the Cape of Good Hope. Yet, despite their arrival, Tippoo persisted in his plans, and sent off an agent, Dubuc, to France. It was the news of his departure from Tranquebar on February 7, which convinced Mornington of the futility of all attempts at conciliating Tippoo [1] ; and his statesmanlike handling of the diplomatic situation, which ensured the help of the Nizam and the neutrality of the Mahrattas, enabled him to take full advantage of the military situation brought about by the operations of sea power.

As happened after the previous wars, the lessons gleaned in 1798–99 influenced the conditions of peace. Unsatisfactory as were most of the terms of the Treaty of Amiens (March 1802), yet the Addington Cabinet insisted on the retention of the Dutch settlements in Ceylon ; and when Grenville and others censured the Addington Cabinet for retroceding the Cape, Pitt during the debates in Parliament declared that the Dutch posts in Ceylon were more important than the Cape for the defence of India. The statement was evidently founded on the experience gained in

[1] Wellesley, " Correspondence," pp. 433, 474, 497.

Suffren's campaigns, as also on the advice sent home by
Mornington.[1]    But in the larger domain of world-strategy
which Bonaparte had opened up, its correctness may be
questioned.    In this connection we may note that, after
the renewal of war, the Pitt Administration despatched a
considerable force in the summer of 1805 over an uncommanded sea for the capture of Cape Town, in order to guard
British India from Napoleon's oriental designs.    This
episode, however, belongs to a period later than that which
can be treated here.    In this article I have striven to show
that from 1746 to 1799 the decisive issue in the struggle for
supremacy in India was that of supremacy at sea.    Clive
summed up only the most obvious features of the problem
in his letter of January 7, 1759, to Pitt :

" The superiority of our squadron, and the plenty of
money and supplies of all kinds which our friends on the
coast will be furnished with from this province [Bengal],
while the enemy are in total want of everything, without
any visible means of redress, are such advantages as, if
properly attended to, cannot fail of wholly effecting their
ruin in that as well as in every other part of India." [2]

[1] Wellesley, "Correspondence," i. 31-33.
[2] Malcolm, " Life of Clive," ii. 119.

# VI

## NAPOLEON AND SEA POWER [1]

THE generally successful result of our naval wars may be ascribed largely to the advancement of experienced seamen to high office at the Admiralty. Since the period of the Dutch Wars this practice has prevailed more here than among our rivals, the outcome being the accumulation of a body of naval doctrine which has proved to be invaluable at crises such as arose in and after 1793. On the other hand, the Revolution in France bore hard on her marine, leading to the emigration of most of the officers, and to the infiltration of doctrinaire views, derived from the land campaigns of 1793.[2] Such, in brief, were the conditions amidst which the young Bonaparte came into contact with the Mediterranean campaign of that year.

Hitherto he seems to have paid little attention to naval history. Yet the note-books in which he summarised his historical studies while at Auxonne in 1789–90 show that he carefully studied and summarised the translation of John Barrow's "New and Impartial History of England" (10 vols. 1762). In that work, compiled at the end of the Seven Years' War, due emphasis is laid on mastery at sea as a factor in our national growth; but in his notes Bonaparte, as was natural in 1789, laid far more stress on political changes and upheavals than on naval wars, allotting twelve times as much space to James I. as to Elizabeth, and dismissing the Spanish Armada very briefly.

---

[1] Reprinted from the "Cambridge Historical Journal" for 1925.
[2] Chevalier, "La Marine française," ii. 24-72.

It is clear, then, that the influence of sea power aroused in him no living interest. Probably it repelled him ; for in his " Lettres sur la Corse," of nearly the same date, he noted that the islanders had no fleet wherewith to beat off invaders, and the thought inspired the following patriotic lament :

" The sea, which for all the other peoples was the first source of riches and power—the sea, which raised Tyre, Carthage, Athens, which still upholds England, Holland, France, etc., in the height of splendour and power—was the source of the misfortunes and misery of my Fatherland." [1]

Clearly, then, his dislike of the sea was not due to ignorance of history ; for he had grasped all that she then had to say on the prime importance of maritime control ; and, though her lessons were not couched in the scientific terms of a Colomb or a Mahan, yet they were unmistakable. His dislike, during this Corsican period of his career, arose from his perception that mastery at sea favoured the great and told against the small peoples. When, however, the French Revolution merged his insular patriotism in that of democratic France, his tone changed. Early in 1793, in his "Mémoire" advocating a second expedition to occupy the Madalena Isles, north-east of Sardinia, he pointed out the strategic advantages of that anchorage (soon to be perceived by Nelson) as enabling France to gain the command of the Mediterranean. Equally significant is it that, even in 1793, he mentions no naval methods of assuring such domination, but implies that it will be assured by the possession of the most commanding posts, constituting an irresistible system of coastal control. Thus early do we see in embryo the policy of the First Consul and Emperor, which appears full-fledged in the Continental System.

Events soon enabled him to test his ideas by practice. The first letter in the official " Correspondance de Napoléon " reveals his perception that the kernel of the Royalist defence of Toulon lay in the supporting fleets of Admirals Hood and

[1] F. Masson, " Napoléon inconnu," ii. 129 ; H. F. Hall, " Napoleon's Notes on English History," p. 9.

Langara.    As commander of the artillery of the Republican
besiegers, he declares his resolve to capture the heights
south of Toulon, and, by driving away the fleets from both
the inner and outer roads, to recover that city for the
Republic.    That design was not a secret revealed to his
genius alone.    It is now known that Lord Hood and our
military commander, Lord Mulgrave, had already seen the
importance of those heights and took steps which for the
present thwarted his efforts.[1]  Ultimately, however, his
persistent attacks succeeded ;  the allied fleets sailed away,
and Toulon fell (December 18).    The episode is of great
importance, for the prolonged artillery duels and the
dramatic finale tended to confirm his belief that the land
dominated the sea.

The sequel clinched that conviction.    The Spanish fleet
went home ;  and Hood's force, worn by the exhausting
service at Toulon, could not stop either the coastwise trade
(which Bonaparte protected by batteries), or delay the
French advance along the Western Riviera.    The British
captured Corsica ;  but Bonaparte counted confidently on
expelling them.    " Let us fight our way along the Riviera
to that post of vantage, Vado Bay, drive away the English
squadron there co-operating with the Austro-Sardinian
defenders, then penetrate into North and Central Italy, and
Corsica will again be ours."    Such is the programme ;  and
the events of 1795–96 crowned it with success.    In this case
Bonaparte's disregard of Britain's naval power was justified.
For the peevish recall of Hood by Earl Spencer led to the
substitution of an inferior commander, Sir William Hotham,
whose lack of enterprise crippled the operations of the
Mediterranean fleet and enfeebled Nelson's light squadron,
based on Vado Bay.    The result was disaster to our Allies
and discredit to us.    The gate of Italy was lost, and through
it Bonaparte drove the wedge which severed our Allies from
one another and from Nelson.[2]

[1] J. H. Rose, " Lord Hood and the Defence of Toulon," p. 42.
[2] Nicolas, " Despatches of Nelson," ii. 46, 59, 61-64, 102-111;
" Spencer Papers," ii. 400.

His estimate of the importance of sea power appeared in one of the conditions now exacted from the beaten court of Turin, viz. the right to garrison the mountain fortress of Coni, which commanded the Col di Tenda pass between Nice and Piedmont. Thereby he not only shortened his communications with Nice but also screened them from naval pressure which even now might have embarrassed him along the Corniche route. Here, as at other points, his strategic conceptions far transcended those of the Maréchal de Maillebois in the same arena. In 1745 the Maréchal, owing to the temporary withdrawal of the British fleet from the Mediterranean, pushed his forces from the Corniche into the heart of Lombardy. Its return to that sea in 1746 cut his communications and compelled him to a retreat along the Corniche, which at Mentone nearly became a disaster.[1] Bonaparte (a close student of Maillebois' campaign) avoided that danger, and his campaign is a perfect example of the trenchant and triumphant use of land power.[2]

Other events told against the British navy. The Spanish declaration of war (October 1796) and the threats of invasion from French, Flemish, and Dutch ports induced the British Government to abandon Corsica and Elba and recall the Mediterranean fleet. Thus within nine months of his beginning the Italian campaign Bonaparte seemed to have assured the final and irreversible predominance of France in the Mediterranean. This brilliant triumph exercised on his mind an impression which was profound and permanent. Yet it was fallacious in that he ignored the temporary and artificial character of the British naval reverse.

In 1797 he garners the fruits of victory. After driving the Austrians from the Peninsula he secures the naval resources of Genoa, Leghorn, Venice, and Corfu. He also compels Victor Amadeus at Turin to promise to cede the Isle of Sardinia at the general pacification. Thereafter, he forces Austria to surrender all claim to the Ionian Isles,

---

[1] Richmond, " The Navy in the War of 1739–48," iii. ch. 6.

[2] I dissent from the main thesis of Gen. Pierron's " Comment s'est formé le génie mil. de Napoléon Ier."

which he warns the Directory are of more importance than
the whole of Italy ; for they border on the Turkish Empire,
now visibly crumbling ; and from those vantage points
France must seize Egypt and destroy Britain's commercial
power, based on the East Indies.[1]

A new phase of activity now opens out. It has often
been pronounced fantastic, yet it rested on the belief that
the Latin combination—France, Spain, and Italy—controlled the Mediterranean, and that its protagonist could
extend to the east the policy of coastal supremacy hitherto
brilliantly successful in the west. Sardinia, Malta, and the
Morea seemed an easy prey. Turkey was a negligible
quantity. The German powers and Russia were digesting
their extensive acquisitions. The British navy, it is true,
had beaten the Spaniards and Dutch at St. Vincent and
Camperdown ; but it was fully occupied by the defence of
its colonies and commerce, and the protection of the coasts
of England and Ireland. An invasion flotilla spread out
from Cherbourg to Flushing aroused fear in London and
wild hopes in Dublin. Therefore on February 14, 1798, so
shrewd a judge as the Foreign Minister, Talleyrand, advised
the Directory that " England cannot intimidate us," and
that an expedition to Egypt would be the best means of
ending the war.[2]

Bonaparte had long been preparing this romantic venture. Probably the two men worked on parallel lines to
assure it. They were on confidential terms ; and nine days
after Talleyrand sent his " Mémoire sur l'Égypte " to the
Directory, Bonaparte wrote a lengthy letter of a similar
tenor. After inspecting the flotilla in the northern ports
he rejected the plan of an invasion of England in a sentence
which even Admiral Mahan could not have improved on :
" To effect an invasion of England without having mastery
at sea is the boldest and most difficult operation which has
been undertaken." The rest of the letter is on the same
high level of political and strategic sagacity. Finally, he

---

[1] " Correspondance," 1912–1915, 1949, 2061, 2072, 2103, 2195.
[2] De la Jonquière, " L'Expédition d'Égypte," i. 154-168.

recommends the Directors to keep up all the appearances of invasion until the navy is able to cover it (as may be the case in 1799) and meanwhile ruin British commerce either by occupying North-West Germany or by an eastern expedition.[1]

An Irish rising being then imminent, and French preparations for succour being in appearance formidable, the British Government seemed unlikely so far to depart from the defensive policy assumed at the end of 1796 as to send a great fleet into the Mediterranean ; and Bonaparte, while ever scouting the thought of going in person to Ireland, clearly based his oriental strategy on the expected French diversion in the north-west. He could not foresee that, after he sailed eastward, the Directory would so far whittle down their Irish efforts as to uncover his rear.[2] He counted on the intimidating effect of some 30 French warships at Brest, 12 Dutchmen at the Texel, and 200 gun-vessels along the French and Flemish coasts ; and even suggested sending 14 French vessels from the Mediterranean to Brest in order to back up the " sure " warfare against the islanders.[3]

Great, then, was his astonishment at the reappearance of a British fleet in the Mediterranean. In truth he had under-estimated the effects of the victories of St. Vincent and Camperdown. The Pitt Ministry, now relieved of immediate fears from the main Spanish and Dutch fleets, was encouraged to brave the risks of invasion, and resolved to send a fleet to that sea ; but Earl Spencer and his Sea Lords regarded the proposal with grave misgivings. So late as April 26 the First Lord pronounced it highly dangerous, adding that, unless our efforts speedily led to a decisive victory, " we must make up our minds to the French dominion of the Mediterranean." [4] It is clear that the demands of Austria for naval support in that quarter

[1] " Correspondance," 2419.

[2] Desbrière, " Projets . . . de débarquement aux Îles britanniques," ii. 50.　　　　　　　　　　　　　　[3] " Correspondance," 2502.

[4] " Spencer Papers," ii. 322.

furnished the arguments for overbearing the scruples of
the Admiralty.

In the new light thrown by the " Spencer Papers " on the
situation in the spring of 1798, the charges of foolhardiness
brought against Bonaparte for venturing to Egypt over
an uncommanded sea must be revised.[1] If on technical
grounds Spencer and his colleagues disapproved the despatch of a British fleet into the Mediterranean, surely
Bonaparte was justified in regarding those waters as fairly
safe.  In point of fact Jervis' despatch thither of Nelson
at first with only three seventy-fours was a venturesome
act, which has been condemned by an acknowledged
authority.[2]  In fact, both sides ran very considerable risks
in May–June, 1798, Bonaparte's being really the greater,
because he was hampered by the presence of nearly 400
transports crowded with troops and had no trustworthy
chart of any roadstead in Egypt.  As is well known,
Nelson's glorious daring changed the course of history.

To Bonaparte the news of the Battle of the Nile came
as a bolt from the blue.  For though, since July 1, he knew
of the presence of a British fleet in those waters, yet he
harboured a feeling of complete security, as his instructions
to his admiral Brueys testify.  On July 3, after the capture
of Alexandria, he ordered him to take the fleet into that
narrow and difficult harbour, or anchor in Aboukir Bay, or
proceed to Corfu.  The soundings at Alexandria being
doubtful, Brueys remained at Aboukir, maintaining that
Bonaparte desired his support on the Egyptian coast.  It
is now known that in the interview of July 4 with his
admiral the commander-in-chief expressed full approval of
the Aboukir station and subsequently sent forty guns to
help strengthen it.[3]  On July 27, Bonaparte, while at
Cairo, expressed a hope that the fleet was in Alexandria.[4]

[1] Chevalier, ii. 358.
[2] Colomb, " Naval Warfare," p. 401.
[3] G. Douin, " La Flotte de Bonaparte sur les côtes d'Égypte "
(Cairo, 1922), pp. 69-74.
[4] Jonquière (ii. 309) shows that this letter (No. 2851 in the official
" Correspondance ") has been altered. He accepts the version in

On July 30, at Cairo, he wrote again, stating that probably
the English were inferior in numbers and were blockading
Malta ; but Brueys must enter Alexandria, take on board
provisions, and then proceed to Corfu, in order to be able
to impose on the Turks.[1]  The provisioning of a large fleet,
however, required time ; and in a letter of August 3 to the
French commander at Corfu he said nothing as to the arrival
of Brueys' fleet.   Probably, then, he did not wish Brueys
to depart, but issued orders which confused the admiral,
and left all the responsibility on his shoulders.[2]   Very noteworthy too is it that in 1807 he sought to destroy the correspondence on this subject,[3] and in his narrative dictated to
Bertrand at St. Helena (" Campagnes d'Égypte et de
Syrie ") threw all the blame for the Aboukir disaster on
Brueys.

Bonaparte's genius never shone more brightly than after
a great reverse.   While admitting to the Directors that the
empire of the sea now belonged to England, he urges them
to strive to unite seven sail at Malta and six at Corfu, in
order to relieve the army of Egypt.   Then he subdues the
natives, founds a naval station at Suez, and sends a bombastic letter to Tippoo Sahib encouraging him to shake
off the iron yoke of England.[4]   Though cut off from France,
he prepares for a spring expedition to Syria, the real object
of which is to overthrow the Turkish army, advancing via
Damascus, before their naval expedition can effect a landing
in Egypt.[5]

Here again he ignored the British fleet.   True, Nelson
had retired, as Bonaparte foresaw ; but a British squadron
was likely to reappear to strengthen the two sail blockading
Alexandria ; and in that case the Syrian venture must fail.
Indeed, if Sir Sidney Smith's squadron had not been long

---

" Copies of the original Letters . . . Intercepted by . . . Lord Nelson "
(London, 1798).

[1] " Correspondance," 2878.

[2] Jonquière, ii. 320-322, 422-428.

[3] Douin, op. cit., ad fin.

[4] " Correspondance," 3045, 3056, 3063, 3901.

[5] Berthier, " Relation . .   de la Campagne d'Égypte," p. 38.

delayed at Constantinople by the ever-deferred promises of
Turkish help, it would have struck at his flank either at
El Arish or Gaza, while the French were wearied by the
desert marches.  As it happened, Smith did not appear
until the French were nearing Acre ; but, clearly, Bonaparte had not expected him at all ; for he had ordered two
flotillas to set out from Damietta and Alexandria, with the
siege train, and, under weak escort, proceed to Haifa.  He
countermanded them when too late.  Off Mount Carmel
Smith captured them almost entire, and turned against the
French their own siege artillery.  The incident was decisive.  After a month of futile efforts against Acre, Bonaparte admitted that he would give 1,000,000 francs for the
lost siege train.[1]  Not until near the end of the sixty-two
days' siege did he receive some heavy guns, and then Turkish
reinforcements were approaching by sea.  It is clear, then,
that naval intervention saved Acre from capture.[2]  Why,
apart from vanity, he persisted so long in that very costly
siege is a mystery ; for in any case he intended to retire
to Egypt.  If, as he claimed, Acre was a necessary base for
the conquest of Syria, his vision, so keen for land warfare,
was at fault ; for Acre occupied a low-lying projection,
easily commanded by ships' guns.  If memories of Toulon
haunted him, the analogy was fallacious ; for there the
land dominated the ships, while at Acre the reverse was the
case.

As for the talk about an Indian campaign, to be undertaken from this untenable base, it sufficed to exalt him,
and to start stimulating discussions whether the campaign
could be accomplished within four months on 50,000 camels
and 10,000 horses through Persia, or by the Red Sea on
frigates taken to pieces and transported to Suez.[3]  The
effect on Kléber was different.  He noted in his diary :

---

[1] " Correspondance," 4091.

[2] Bertrand, *op. cit.* ii. 94.  Jonquière (iv. 637) underrates the naval
factor at Acre.

[3] Bertrand, i. 123 ; Desvernois, " Méms.," 148 ; Gourgaud, " Journal
inédit de Ste. Hélène," ii. 74, 315.

" Jamais de plan fixe : sa qualité c'est d'oser et d'oser encore : et il va dans cet art jusqu'au delà de la témérité."

The naval problems confronting Bonaparte after his escape to France were very complex. The British, besides weakening the Dutch navy, had occupied Minorca and were blockading the French forces in Malta and Egypt, while the armies of the Second Coalition threatened France herself. Her perils being due to his oriental adventure, it behoved him, after beating the Austrians, to strive to relieve his troops in Valetta and the valley of the Nile. But, the Toulon fleet having been destroyed by Nelson, the burden now rested with the Brest fleets, consisting of 17 French and 15 Spanish sail. The problem was to elude the close British blockade, to drive away or capture the blockaders of Cadiz, to unite with the Spanish force, and then fall upon the British squadrons scattered over the Mediterranean. In this snowball strategy the First Consul showed much ingenuity. He early insisted on the equipment of the combined fleet at Brest and of light squadrons elsewhere for the speedy relief of Valetta. His correspondence in the year 1800 reveals the merits and defects of his procedure—on the one side, boundless energy, inspiring patriotism, and an unshakable resolve to retain Malta and Egypt ; on the other, an imperious and exacting will that rarely realises and never allows for the limitations then besetting the discouraged and half-starved French naval service.[1] Above all, he fails to understand why 32 ships cannot beat out of Brest against the prevailing westerly winds and drive away half their number of storm-tossed craft clinging to the dangerous offing of Ushant.

After the Marengo campaign he redoubles his efforts, and on July 13 orders the warships at Brest, Lorient, and Rochefort to be ready for sea within five weeks, mapping out their proceedings—the junction with the Spanish squadrons, and the relief or capture of Malta, Minorca, and

[1] " Correspondance," 4612, 4618, 4625, 4637, 4653, 4675 ; Chevalier, iii. 47 ; Leyland, " Blockade of Brest," i. p. 11.

Alexandria. Great is his chagrin when none of them can stir. Not until January 1801 does Rear-Admiral Ganteaume with seven sail get clear away from Brest during a favouring gale, which, however, so batters them that he finally makes for Toulon. There, watched and dogged by Admiral Warren, he fails to land a man in Egypt. Valetta meanwhile has fallen to the Union flag, which thenceforth controls the Mediterranean. As for the twenty months' blockade of Brest by an inferior force, Bonaparte pronounces it " shameful and humiliating to both nations." [1] Humiliating it was : shameful it was not, in view of the difficulty of working out of that port in face of a fleet marshalled by St. Vincent or Cornwallis.

Repeated checks only lead him to stress his policy of diversions. They are fourfold—imposing naval preparations from the Texel to Genoa, the menace of an invasion of England, the extinction of our last ally, Portugal, and encouragement to the League of the Armed Neutrals. In this league he places great hopes, and on January 27, 1801, writes confidently to Talleyrand that he intends to exclude the British from the Continent and undertake great expeditions either to Ireland or Brazil and India [sic] or Surinam, Trinidad, etc., or " several expeditions in the Mediterranean." [2] The letter is significant. Ignoring the lessons of the long and effective British blockades of Brest and Cadiz, and confident of the success of his policy of diversions, he pictures the enemy retiring on their own coasts, while Franco-Spanish-Dutch squadrons range the seas at will. A fortnight later, after compelling Austria and Naples to a peace, he spurs on the Spaniards to prepare at once fifteen sail for the support of an equal number of French in the Mediterranean, and foretells that, as the English are now excluded from Italy and Sicily, they must abandon that sea.

Again, then, he relies on land pressure to drive out an isolated fleet. Also, after the collapse of his Portuguese and Armed Neutrality schemes, he urges on the invasion

[1] " Lettres inédites," 11, 13, 21.　　[2] " Correspondance," 5327.

flotilla.   For months he has ordered construction in all the
ports from Antwerp to Quiberon, under the command of
Admiral Latouche-Tréville.   That seaman, eagerly entering
into the idea of invasion, makes light of the difficulties of
concentrating the swarm of small craft at Boulogne, of
getting most of them out of harbour in one tide, and of
crossing over to Romney Marsh or Rye.   Admitting the
obstacles caused by the differences in size and stability of
the boats, the cramped space at Boulogne, and the strength
of the tides in the Straits, he yet pronounces the passage
feasible in ten hours of calm.   On this one occasion Bonaparte is less hopeful than his chief Admiral.   More than
once he checks his *élan* and keeps him strictly to the
defensive.[1]   Also, on June 23, 1801, he writes to General
Augereau, commanding the French forces in Holland,
urging him to prepare for sea the Dutch part of the flotilla
" in order that we may impose on England." [2]

The phrase explains much.   It implies that he uses the
flotilla as a means of intimidating the Addington Ministry
now in power at Westminster.   There is not a word in his
letters of 1800–01 that implies a resolve actually to attempt
the crossing.   Thiers describes him as stating confidentially
to the two other Consuls that, if he cannot procure good
terms of peace from England, he will complete his flotilla,
embark 100,000 men on it, and risk life, glory, and fortune in
an invasion.   Over against *ce beau geste* one may place the
following facts :   (1) The flotilla is far from complete ;   and
it must now carry horses for the cavalry and artillery, seeing
that the English plans for sweeping bare the coast districts
are complete.   (2) Up to mid-September 1801 the western
divisions have not concentrated at Boulogne, and now
cannot with safety, owing to the weather.   (3) Several of
the larger units have to be kept moored outside Boulogne at
considerable risk for lack of harbour space.   (4) So late as
May 19, 1801, he orders extensive works that will enable *all*
the flotilla to shelter in that harbour.   In September these

[1] Desbrière, ii. 296-298, 307, 309, 393.
[2] " Correspondance," 5617.

are scarcely begun. (5) He believes that the crossing is feasible only in the long nights.[1] Yet he begins to press on the negotiations for peace seriously on September 17, *i.e.* at the season when long nights are beginning. His motive is to close quickly with England before she hears the news of the surrender of the French garrison at Alexandria.

The drift of it all is clear. Egypt was his great preoccupation. To save that cherished colony, he stirred up trouble for England at Lisbon, in the Baltic, and in the Straits of Dover. The distractions proved to be unavailing ; for every action of the British Admiralty, at Copenhagen, in the Mediterranean, above all, in the dogged maintenance of the Brest and Cadiz blockades, showed a complete penetration of his purpose.[2] In such a case, to keep up a game of bluff is useless, and he wisely ended the war while he could do so to advantage, trusting that what force had failed to extort from the British navy could be gained by finesse from Addington.

Herein he succeeded ; for he had a naval policy, while the Addington Cabinet had none, and therefore lost on paper what had been won at sea. It consented to give up the chief strategic gains of the war—St. Lucia, Cape Town, Minorca, and Malta (the last to the impotent Knights of St. John).[3] Consequently Napoleon soon resumed his Mediterranean schemes, annexing Piedmont, Parma, and Elba, and revealing his design once more to occupy Egypt and the Ionian Isles. War broke out in May 1803, ostensibly on the Maltese question, really on the larger issues which it involved.[4] His rage at the interruption to

---

[1] Desbrière, ii. pt. iii. chaps. 1-4 ; "Correspondance," 2419, 7309.

[2] St. Vincent and Nelson in July 1801 took the French preparations for invasion seriously ; but the latter, after further experience, pronounced them impossible, from Boulogne. ("Letters of Lord St. Vincent," p. 125 ; Nicolas, iv. 425-427, 438, 443-447, 482.)

[3] St. Vincent pushed party discipline to an extreme in his assertion ("Letters," i. 285) that the peace was the best ever made by England. She gave up her maritime gains except Trinidad and Ceylon, ceded by Spain and Holland. France, while retaining her military conquests, received back all her colonies.

[4] "Camb. Hist. of Brit. Foreign Policy," i. 310-327.

his pacific aggressions is explained by one of his private declarations, that he expected to resume war some eighteen months later. For the present, as his naval preparations were backward, he threw himself into the preparations for invasion by the flotilla.[1] Secondary means of coercing England were the occupation of Hanover and of South Italy, with the aim of dispersing her naval forces more widely and confusing the British Admiralty.

All was in vain. That body, recovering from the weaknesses that marked its conduct in 1794-96, now recurred to the sound system of the days of Anson and Hawke, that of blockading the chief enemy fleets.[2] Brest, Toulon (Cadiz also when Spain came into the war), were carefully watched, and the lures of Napoleon proved to be unavailing. As always happened when his will was thwarted, he piled threat upon threat, mass upon mass. In May 1803 he ordered 310 new units for the flotilla to be completed, first by Christmas, then to be hurried on and be ready by September 23 ; next, on July 5, he ordered 1410 units : on August 22 the number rose to 2008 (inclusive of commandeered fishing-boats) estimated to carry 97,000 troops, 17,000 non-combatants, and 7094 horses, besides cannon, stores, and food.[3] No time was specified for this latest programme, apparently because at least two years were needed for the completion of the necessary harbour works at Ambleteuse, Wimereux, Boulogne, and Étaples. To the last place Napoleon persisted in sending vessels of too great draught, most of which remained useless there.[4] The immense orders of vessels, from the *prames* to the little *péniches*, and the cost and care bestowed on their armament prove that during several weeks he hoped that the flotilla would fight its way across to Kent or would at least cause a panic in England.

---

[1] O. Browning, " England and Napoleon," pp. 80, 100, 174.
[2] Leyland, " Blockade of Brest," ii. Introduction and pp. 48-50; Corbett, " Campaign of Trafalgar," ch. i.
[3] Desbrière, iii. 83, 84, 94, 106.
[4] *Ibid.* iii. 469.

Whether in the year 1803 he designed the flotilla as his main striking force or as a temporary means of reducing us to the defensive until his new fleets were ready, is open to question. His nature ever prompted him to a swift and daring offensive. Pride, ambition, and sensitiveness to the *persiflage* of the boulevards also forbade the lengthy preparations which sound naval strategy prescribed. On the other hand, he saw clearly the risks of invasion by the flotilla. In February 1803, during one of his outbursts to Whitworth, British ambassador at Paris, he asked fiercely what he had to gain by a rupture with Great Britain ; for the flotilla, his only means of offence, involved risks of a hundred to one against him ; but army after army would be found for the enterprise, which his honour compelled him to attempt.[1] The blend of frankness and menace is characteristic. On the whole it seems probable that the vast preparations for a crossing by the flotilla alone were only an effort to reduce us to the defensive—always his leading purpose in war. The threat became serious only when the French, Dutch, and Spanish fleets attained, on paper, equality with our own. Then the flotilla was reduced to its proper function, that of a ferry, needing strong escort after the hostile fleets were driven or decoyed away.

Thenceforth the problem resembled that which confronted the Spanish Armada and the admirals of Louis XIV. and XV. The British fleet having been disposed of for a time, the Spanish or French squadrons from the ocean ports had to pick up the transports and light craft from the cramped harbours of Picardy and Flanders, convoy them to the almost harbourless coasts opposite, and guard their communications until the English Government surrendered. The enormous complexity of the problem is obvious. In no important effort since 1066 has even the first condition been thoroughly fulfilled. At one time Napoleon came nearer to a solution than his predecessors ; but, as he had not studied their efforts adequately, he underrated the difficulties inherent in the enterprise, as will now appear.

[1] O. Browning, " England and Napoleon," p. 100.

By the end of 1803 there are clear signs that he intended
to throw the chief burden on the French and Allied fleets
now feverishly being prepared by Decrès, Minister of Marine.
On December 7 the First Consul asked the advice of
Ganteaume, now maritime prefect at Toulon, concerning
three alternative plans of action for the Toulon fleet of nine
sail, to which he assigned the initiative.  In all three
versions Ganteaume is assumed to put to sea on January 11,
1804, then, by alternative means to rally the Rochefort
squadron of seven sail and so arrive off Boulogne in April
(*c'est un peu tard*).  Meanwhile the Brest fleet is to be ready
with troops on board to proceed towards the north-west,
thereby throwing Cornwallis off the scent towards Ireland,
and gaining three days on him.  It too will appear before
Boulogne, where the First Consul will be ready to embark
on the flotilla with 130,000 men.[1]  As an afterthought, he
asks :  " Can twenty sail easily get out of Brest ? "—as
though all the previous experiences had not demonstrated
the contrary, except during a strong easterly gale, which
drove away the blockaders.

This phantasmagoria receiving its quietus from Ganteaume, the destination of the Toulon fleet is suddenly
changed to Martinique, now reported to be in danger.[2]
Indeed, it is noteworthy that, along with feverish preparations of the flotilla and constant nautical exercises prescribed for the blockaded fleets, he intends if possible to
save from capture the French, Dutch, and Spanish West
Indies.  Finally he assigns that task to the French squadron
which, in breach of the laws of neutrality, is undergoing
lengthy repairs at Ferrol.[3]  The grand enterprise against
England is reserved to the fleets at Toulon, Rochefort,
and Brest.

After the assumption of the Imperial title in May 1804,

[1] Colomb ("Naval Warfare," p. 185) says that not till May 8, 1805,
did Napoleon aim at securing the naval command of the Channel ; but
it is clearly stipulated on December 7, 1803.
[2] " Correspondance," 7359, 7442 ; Desbrière, iii. 636-639.
[3] *Ibid.* 7842.

every fleet, every dockyard, every port in Picardy and
Flanders feels the impact of his impetuous will.  Work of
fourteen hours a day is enjoined, and by July 1804 he
counts on having 1800 units ready to embark 120,000 troops
and 10,000 horses—" Let us be masters of the Strait for six
hours and we shall be masters of the world." [1]  Here it may
be noted that in the letter of July 20, 1805 (when all was
ready at Boulogne), he extended the necessary time of
respite in the Channel to three days, and in his post mortem
defence of the flotilla policy (September 13, 1805) to fifteen
days.[2]  Apparently in this last (surely designed for posterity)
he at last confronted the necessity, not only of landing, but
also of capturing London and exacting peace before Nelson
and Cornwallis returned and cut off his communications.
For, be it observed, his invasion plans of 1804–5 aimed only
at securing temporary evasion of Britain's sea power, not at
mastery of the sea, which, in February 1798 he stipulated
as essential to success.

Certainly, if the sudden concentration of a nation's force,
of engineering skill, of a marvellous organisation, and of an
imperious will on a naval problem could have compelled
success, it would have been his.  This plan of July 1804,
as explained to Latouche-Tréville, now commanding the
Toulon fleet, is very ingenious.  At all costs that admiral
must complete for sea the 10 sail now at Toulon.  Then,
waiting for *un bon mistral* to blow away Nelson's look-out
frigates, and send him scudding eastwards after the Italo-
Egyptian lure, he is to bear the tricolour in triumph to the
ocean.  Thereupon, after a wide sweep westwards, he will
appear at Rochefort, pick up five sail, and, repeating the
manœuvre off Brest, liberate that fleet, and thus arrive in
force off Boulogne in September.[3]

Such is the plan ;  probably the best of all Napoleon's
naval combinations.  It errs, however, in supposing, first,
that Nelson will long grope about the Levant ;  and that the
British squadrons off Rochefort and Brest will be as
inert as Beaulieu's starchy array was under the blows of

[1] " Correspondance," 7832.        [2] *Ibid.* 8998, 9209.        [3] *Ibid.* 7832.

Napoleon's eager youth.   Moreover, Latouche-Tréville died
six weeks later, and with him disappeared the dash and
energy of the old French navy.   Therefore the plan was
never put to the test.

In March 1805 died Bruix, commander of the naval
forces at Boulogne.   Whether he believed in the practic-
ability of the invasion scheme is doubtful ; for in his letter
of August 31, 1804, to Talleyrand he complains of endless
difficulties thrown in his way and of Napoleon's suspicions
as to his half-heartedness.   On two recent occasions he had
ventured to cross the Emperor's will.   In the latter case he
persistently refused to order a review of the flotilla when a
gale was brewing.   In a fit of fury Napoleon raised his
riding-whip as if to strike Bruix, whose hand flew to his
sword.   After an angry glare the Emperor turned on his
heel ; but he ordered Rear-Admiral Magon, second in
command, to carry out his instruction.   Magon weakly
consented.   As the review was beginning, the storm burst ;
eight vessels foundered, and between 50 and 100 lives were
sacrificed to the Emperor's demand for implicit obedience.[1]
This incident and others like it remind us that we are dealing
with an abnormal personage, whose inexperience in matters
nautical by no means led him to defer to the ripe judgement
of experts.

Limits of space preclude a survey of the other invasion
schemes except the last, that of March 2, 1805.   Spain
having come into the war, Napoleon now uses her Cadiz
fleet, though very rawly manned, to reinforce that of
Toulon, commanded by Villeneuve.   That admiral, after
escaping from Toulon (if possible by March 15) and throwing
Nelson eastwards off the scent, will drive away the British
from off Cadiz, rally the Spanish squadron under Gravina,
and proceed with the combined fleet to the West Indies.
There, after doing what damage he can to the enemy, and
landing troops at the French stations, he will at Martinique
wait not more than forty days for Ganteaume's fleet from
Brest.   To Ganteaume with 21 sail is assigned the task

[1] Nicolay, " Napoléon au Camp de Boulogne," ch. ix.

of setting free the French and Spanish ships blockaded at Ferrol. Thereupon he will take the chief command after the junction at Martinique, where Admiral Missiessy with five sail from Rochefort is expected also to be *en rade*. If Ganteaume does not arrive within forty days, Villeneuve will proceed to Santiago Bay in the Canaries (a bay which he could find on no map [1]), there wait for him twenty days, and then proceed to Cadiz for further orders. Villeneuve's cruise (Napoleon hints) may change the destinies of the world ; but only to Ganteaume and General Lauriston is confided the secret, that, if all goes well, the combined fleets are to return direct to Ushant, overpower the British squadron, and between June 10 and July 10 gloriously crown the grand design in the Straits of Dover. [2]

Napoleon's chief aims, then, are twofold, (1) the destruction of British West India commerce, and the strengthening of the French, Spanish, and Dutch West Indies ; (2) the muster at Martinique of an overpowering fleet, which will return, sweep the Channel, and convoy the flotilla. His choice of so distant a rendezvous as Martinique has been explained by the resolve to attain secrecy and to exercise the long beleaguered French and Spanish crews before the final test off Dover. But his correspondence shows the increasing importance which he assigned to the West Indies, [3] and that with the invasion scheme he now associated a West India scheme. If his aim had been merely evasion of Nelson and Cornwallis, a junction at one of the Azores or the Canaries would have answered the purpose better. As it was, he greatly overburdened his *personnel*, now deteriorating after two years in harbour, and, as we shall see, prescribed exacting duties for them in that trying climate. Further, the addition of six old and slow Spaniards hopelessly deranged the precise timetable composed at Paris. Accordingly Nelson, though at first lured away eastwards (as Napoleon very skilfully

---

[1] Chevalier, iii. 152.
[2] " Correspondance," 8379–8383.
[3] *Ibid.* 8060, 8206, 8231, 8292, 8309, 8575, 8582, 8618, 8730

planned), nearly caught up Villeneuve and thus shielded the British West Indies. Meanwhile Missiessy was on his way back to Rochefort ; while Ganteaume, the brain of the enterprise, was held fast at Brest. This was not his fault. On March 24 he telegraphed by semaphore to the Emperor his expectation of getting out and beating Cornwallis, but received the immediate reply that such a success would lead to nothing, and he must await an occasion for a sortie without fighting.[1] Theoretically, the argument was correct ; in practice, as against Cornwallis, it marred the whole campaign.

By degrees Napoleon came to see that much time would elapse before Ganteaume eluded Cornwallis. On April 13 he ordered Magon with two sail to steal out of Rochefort and carry orders to Villeneuve not to go to the (hypothetical) Bay of Santiago, but, after conquering a West India island, proceed " straight as an arrow " to Ferrol, beat off the blockaders and release fifteen French and Spanish ships with a view to a similar *coup* at Brest—and Boulogne. As usual in Napoleon's eager brain, this later scheme led to another. During the spring splendours of his Italian progress, he ordered Villeneuve to fill up the time of waiting in the West Indies by taking St. Vincent, Antigua, Grenada (*et pourquoi ne prendrait-on pas la Barbade ?* [2]). Then he pictured the sorties of his squadrons as alarming the British for India, and concluded (May 29) that " the theatre of war is fixed for the East Indies, or England, or Jamaica." Further to confuse the British Admiralty, he commanded Missiessy (now home from Martinique) to put out again and insult the Irish coast, which would serve to withdraw six ships from Cornwallis—*et mon but est rempli*.[3] Again he commented on the short-sightedness and gullibility of that body in sending squadrons about on mere rumours.[4]

[1] *Ibid.* 8480. This order explains Ganteaume's avoidance of battle on July 21, 1805, for which he has been unjustly blamed. (Clowes, " Royal Navy," v. p. vii.)

[2] *Ibid.* 8577, 8618, 8582-8583 ; Desbrière, iv. 503-528.

[3] *Ibid.* 8809.          [4] *Ibid.* 8713, 8938.

There was no sign of flurry at Whitehall. First Lord Melville and then Lord Barham perceived that, so long as Brest, Rochefort, and Ferrol were blockaded, the Boulogne flotilla could not move. As for Villeneuve and Gravina, Nelson would find and hold them. Accordingly (except in one case) the main British fleets were not dispersed or seriously weakened for long [1] ; and, as we shall see, British admirals, when in doubt, fell back on Cornwallis's fleet off Ushant, the pivoting point of British strategy. It was Napoleon who finally ordered excentric moves that over-tasked his admirals. Even the original plan of March 2 was too complex to succeed against experienced and vigilant enemies, but its later annexes border on the fantastic. Naval even more than military operations require simple and direct methods. On land, wherever possible, Napoleon operated along a single line, and left enveloping moves to the Austrians. It therefore passes comprehension that he, who in December 1805 dealt the trenchant stroke of Austerlitz, should, a few months earlier, have planned the overthrow of England by a far-flung and bifurcating scheme.

Nevertheless, when shorn of its West India frills, that scheme narrowly failed of success. For Villeneuve and Gravina, pursued by Nelson, cut short that part of Napoleon's programme, immensely to his advantage, and made sail for Europe. Off Cape Finisterre, on July 22, they lost two ships to Calder's slightly inferior force, and finally put in to Corunna, there rallying the Ferrol squadron. They now had 29 sail, 15 being slow and burdened with sick after the tropical cruise, while the Ferrol crews were slack from the long blockade. So many accidents and collisions occurred in getting out that Villeneuve wrote to Decrès : "A couple of squalls have crippled us because we have bad masts, bad sails, bad rigging, bad officers, and bad sailors." [2] Accordingly he and Gravina, after putting

---

[1] Leyland, ii. 240-338 ; "Mems. of Collingwood," pp. 100-110 ; Desbrière, iv. 480-502, 802-808.

[2] Troude, "Batailles navales," iii. 359.

to sea and meeting with more mishaps and threatening
news as to large hostile forces to the northward, decided
on the 15th to reverse course and make for Cadiz.

Excuses can be urged for this retreat from the scene
of action ; but the fact remains that it paralysed Napoleon's
plan of invasion, and that, too, only a few days after
victory seemed nearly within his grasp. For it so happened
that, on the very day of Villeneuve's sortie from Ferrol
with 29 sail, Cornwallis could muster only 15 off Brest, the
Admiralty having lately withdrawn three sail to strengthen
the squadron at the Downs. Also in Bertheaume Roads,
outside of Brest, Ganteaume with 21 was only waiting for
a favourable wind to put out and demolish him. Napoleon
was now eagerly enjoining the offensive in case the blockaders
had fewer than 16 sail, and ordered Ganteaume then either
to join Villeneuve and sweep the Channel, or, failing that,
to crush the blockaders of Ferrol and rally the Franco-
Spanish squadron at that port. " If (he wrote on July
20) the enemy reduces his force before you, it is because he
is convinced that the offensive must come from Admiral
Villeneuve. Deceive him by yourself taking the initiative.
. . . Be prudent, but also be bold." [1]

The reasoning was worthy of the Emperor. What then
vitiated it ? Merely the weather conditions long prevalent
off Brest which held Ganteaume fast and lessened Cornwallis's keen anxieties off that port.[2] Also the long delay
of the combined fleet in Corunna robbed it of the chance
of meeting the Rochefort squadron of five sail, then
cruising in the Bay, and so falling on Cornwallis with
overwhelming force, 34 on 15. On few occasions have
accidents and weather conditions more deranged the plans
of our would-be invaders, and that too, at a time when
their chances were good. Indeed, it must be admitted
that the British Admiralty, in detaching three sail from
Cornwallis's pivoting force of only 18, in order to strengthen

---

[1] " Correspondance," 8998.

[2] Leyland, ii. 330, 337. Mahan, writing before the publication of these
volumes, did not know of the risk to Cornwallis on August 4-13, 1805.

the Downs squadron against reported movements of the Dutch fleet, was playing a risky game. Cornwallis twice warned them of his weakness after August 4 ; and not until the reinforcements of Stirling, Calder, and Nelson reached him on the 13th–15th, did a very critical situation terminate in our favour. The fact that the Admiralty withdrew three sail from Cornwallis in order to confront the Dutch ships reveals its nervousness as to the menace from the east. It would seem, then, that Napoleon's worst mistake at this time lay in his insufficient use of the Dutch and Flemish naval forces. Formidable demonstrations from the Texel and Flushing in July would have compelled the Admiralty to weaken still further our naval forces in the Ocean, thereby leaving them exposed to a heavy blow. It is significant that the only successful invasion of England by a declared enemy, that of 1066, was preluded by a powerful effort against our long and exposed east coast ; and if Napoleon, instead of indulging in dreams of West India conquests, had prepared a Dutch-Flemish expedition against that coast (analogous to that of Hardrada), the history of the world might well have been different.

As it was, the combined fleet was so clogged by the results of its West India expedition as to be inefficient at the crisis, a fact which partly excuses Villeneuve's retirement to Cadiz. In point of fact he had missed his opportunity by about five days ; for by the time that he turned tail, the arrival of reinforcements brought Cornwallis's total up to 40, of which 9 or 10 were three-deckers ; and that admiral was able to send back Calder with 20 to look after Villeneuve and Ferrol, keeping 19 (for the " Victory " went home) to check Ganteaume. Thus, on August 15 Napoleon's invasion scheme collapsed. It collapsed, partly owing to its imperial top-hamper, but still more owing to the sound judgement of the British admirals in the Atlantic. Their actions were based on the sea lore of the age of Anson and Hawke, which may be summarised thus : " When in doubt, fall back on the central fleet off Ushant, so as to cover the Channel."

Nevertheless Napoleon's naval combinations are not to be dismissed as wholly chimerical. Early in August he might well expect to outwit the British blockaders at some point ; for they then had in the ocean only 50 ships to his 70[1] ; and, if Villeneuve's and Gravina's fleets had been efficient, they should have broken the blockade at Brest, certainly so far as to set free Ganteaume, whereupon his 21 should have liberated the Boulogne flotilla. Setting aside the West India excrescence, Napoleon's project of March 2, 1805, had some merits, and it came far nearer to success than has been allowed by English writers. He failed, partly because he overtaxed an inefficient instrument, the combined fleets, which at the crisis bent under the strain ; but also because he and his admirals were beginners in the great game at which Barham, Nelson, Cornwallis, and Collingwood were past masters, primed with the experience of a century.

On August 22, 1805, Decrès earnestly begged him not to order Villeneuve and Gravina to proceed from Cadiz to the Channel[2] ; and probably it was this remonstrance, no less than Austria's armaments, which weakened the Emperor's resolve to go on with the scheme of invasion. His recent aggressions in Italy had provided the alternative of a Continental war into which he now threw himself with ardour. But, as he clung to a maritime offensive up to August 22, I cannot accept the explanation that his last plan of invasion was designed merely to frighten England and lure Austria into a premature campaign.[3]

That the Emperor himself subsequently put forward this justification of his conduct in subjecting France to the heavy expense of the flotilla was of course to be expected. But this plausible pretext fails to explain the following facts : (1) Not until August 22 is there any hint in his letters as to the abandonment of the invasion project.

---

[1] Desbrière, " La Campagne maritime de 1805," pp. 74-79.

[2] For Decrès' doubts and hesitations see Desbrière, *op. cit.* p. 113.

[3] Desbrière, " Projets, etc.," iii. 372 ; iv. 830 ; v. 398, 465 ; James, " Naval History," iii. 328.

By that time circumstances made him waver ; but up to August 20 he had issued orders to Ganteaume enjoining a sortie and the fulfilment of the grand design if the conditions permitted; and he still believed that the maritime situation was in his favour.   (2) Even so late as August 24 he sent off to Berlin offers of a Franco-Prussian alliance (baited with Hanover) provided that that Court would make armed demonstrations to keep Austria quiet and leave him free for the invasion of England.   (3) He had taken great pains to keep in good repair the roads from Paris to Boulogne and Brest ; but not until August 25th did he order Murat to proceed from Paris to Mainz and survey the roads leading into Bavaria.[1]   During the forced marches which led up to the brilliant victory at Ulm the French troops, as is now known, suffered considerably from lack of food ;  and other signs in that Swabian campaign bespeak a sudden change of plan.

On the other side, it is urged by Méneval,[2] the Emperor's secretary, that now, as always, he made his plans in two ways, and, while seeming to aim at Kent, was in reality preparing for a campaign on the Danube.   This explanation may hold good for the two or three days of balancing after August 22 [3] ; but it cannot apply to the preceding days ; for he was then spurring on Ganteaume and Villeneuve to fight their way through to Boulogne.   What figure would he, the newly-crowned Emperor, have cut if he and his troops had left Boulogne just before his fleets arrived ? Not until August 25, on realising the failure of his naval projects, did he definitely decide for the land campaign.[4] Thenceforth he threw himself into it with triumphant energy, flinging back the taunt that, when France had two or three admirals willing to die, the English would be found to be quite small.[5]

As for the argument that the invasion of England was

---

[1] " Correspondance," 9132.   See, too, 9122.
[2] " Méneval Méms.," i. 407.
[3] " Correspondance," 9133.
[4] Ibid. 9135.          [5] Ibid. 9160.

never seriously intended, it is applicable to an ordinary leader. It is inapplicable to Napoleon. The man who, as general, madly dared and lost at Acre is not to be judged by conventional standards of tame probability when, full blown with pride, he wielded the resources of a vast Empire.

In truth the Napoleonic spirit and the sea spirit are incommensurable. The one is rigid, the other infinitely adaptable. The one is exacting, the other tolerant. The one is derived from the Roman legions, the other from Norse, Dutch, and English sailors. Napoleon was too much of a Caesar ever to make a thoroughly good seaman. Born and bred in the Mediterranean, he was ever thalassic in outlook. Never could he school himself to allow margins for the haze and fog, the tides and currents of the Channel and Ocean. He planned the movements of fleets almost as if they were armies, assuring Neil Campbell at Elba that he had made all his calculations for a landing in England and reduced it to a perfect certainty.[1] Among his naval plans those for the Mediterranean were by far the best ; for there the land largely controlled the sea, and his coastal policy in that sphere attained not only grandiosity but solidity. Even there, however, he erred by excess, and it is significant that in October 1805 he hounded forth Villeneuve and Gravina to almost certain doom rather than witness the consolidation of British influence in his own preserve. Then, as always, when pitted against the heirs of a sound maritime tradition, he lost his mental balance.

After Trafalgar the theme declines in interest ; and it must suffice to note that at intervals his old obsessions reappear. In particular he never realised fully the power of an army based on a fleet. During the Peninsular War he issued orders for driving the British into the sea, forgetting the lesson of Corunna, that an army retreating on its mobile base has great advantages over pursuers operating from Madrid or Bayonne. Wellington early perceived those advantages, to which he finally ascribed the successful

[1] Neil Campbell, " Napoleon . . . at Elba," pp. 229, 339.

issue of that struggle.[1] Neither did Napoleon in 1812 reckon on the disturbing effect of British naval pressure on his sea-borne supplies and on his operations against Riga.[2] Finally, in the summer of 1813, when his Germanic system was tottering, he ordered the construction of a dockyard at Hamburg with a view to " a vast plan of war against England " in 1814.[3] Thus once again emerges the congenital notion of assuring command of the sea from dominating positions on land. But by this time it had assumed megalomaniac proportions.

[1] " Journals of Admiral T. Byam Martin," ii. 409.
[2] *Ibid.* ii. 240, 278, 290-292 ; Ross, " Life of Admiral Saumarez," ii. ch. 13.
[3] " Correspondance," 20150, 20205, 20243.

# VII

## THE PROPHETIC INSTINCT IN NELSON

WAS it not Wellington who said that his chief preoccupation was to find out what the enemy were doing
on the other side of that hill ?   The saying puts in a pithy
and concrete way the duty of a commander, first to get news,
and then to infer what it means.   Obviously sound judgement and imagination are essential for framing a conclusion
as to the enemy's plans ; and the great commander is he who
knows whether caution or boldness should dictate his action.

The warrior's foresight is merely imagination raised to
the $n$th degree by the fire of genius.   It is never divorced
from actuality ;  but, working upon ascertained facts, it
fuses them into an intellectual effort which soars above
actuality.   The greatest victories, both on sea and on land,
were due to something more than sound judgement.   Drake's
dash on Cadiz, Blake's on Santa Cruz, Marlborough's attacks
at Blenheim and Oudenarde, Napoleon's at Rivoli and
Austerlitz, Nelson's at St. Vincent, the Nile and Trafalgar,
did not defy the lessons of experience ;  they extended and
glorified them.

It is futile to inquire whence these warriors derived their
priceless gift of inspired daring.   The only instance of its
exercise recorded in the life of Nelson's father is when that
usually rather timid old rector found a housebreaker in
the rectory at Burnham Thorpe and promptly seized him
by the collar, apparently with no untoward result.[1]
Further, the Rev. Edmund Nelson was Fellow of Gonville

[1] M. E. Matcham, " The Nelsons of Burnham Thorpe," p. 24.

and Caius College, Cambridge, an honour which implied intellectual eminence.   Concerning his consort far less is known than about that Spartan-willed Letizia Ramolino, who dowered Napoleon with his world-compelling qualities. In the case of both heroes we cannot explain the efflorescence of extraordinary gifts.   For all the disquisitions on heredity, genius remains a baffling factor.   Of Napoleon's brothers, only Joseph took up soldiering, which ended at Vittoria. As for Horatio's brothers, they were mediocre landsmen.

Foresight is a plant of slow growth ; and not until Nelson's thirty-fifth year, when he became captain of H.M.S. "Agamemnon," of the Mediterranean fleet, are there clear signs of the emergence of that faculty.   It blossomed quickly under the stimulus of his admiration for stout old Hood, of whom he wrote : "Upwards of seventy, he possesses the mind of a man of forty."   That ever pugnacious Admiral not only fired Nelson with ambition, but, discerning in him a kindred soul, sent him on difficult duties to Naples, Corsica, Tunis, which quickened his political sense.   Full soon the captain judged that we should do little at Toulon and along the Riviera without a large landing force [1] ; and within four months our hurried evacuation of Toulon justified his forecast.   Into the next enterprise, the ejection of the French from Corsica, he threw himself with intense ardour, and expressed unjustifiable scorn for the slowness of our soldiers.   Taking the initiative with a large landing party, he and Lieutenant Duncan threw up batteries which, from the end of March 1794, harassed the French defenders of Bastia.   On May 1 he wrote : "Bastia will be ours between the 20th and 24th of this month, if succours do not get in."   The place did surrender to Hood on May 22, just before our regular troops arrived from S. Fiorenzo.   Despite the loss of the sight of one eye during the siege of Cabri, his indomitable hopefulness persisted, and he foretold with fair accuracy the fall of the place a week after our batteries opened fire.[2]

[1] Sir H. Nicolas, "Despatches of Nelson," i. p. 320.
[2] *Ibid.* i. p. 456.

These experiences on land further widened his outlook. In the autumn of 1794 the French Republicans were pushing along the Italian Riviera, the operations of the British fleet, now under Hotham, being lethargic in the extreme. Nelson's dissatisfaction with that commander led him to express privately the fear that the French would seize that excellent anchorage, Vado Bay, west of Savona, occupy the easy pass north-west of that town, and then easily overrun the plain of Italy. How remarkable are the following prophecies! On September 27, 1794: "I have but little doubt, if the enemy turn their thoughts to the invasion of Italy, that next spring they will accomplish it." Again, on November 28: "Port Especia (Spezzia) is their object, I am convinced; and if they get it, they will plague us more than ever [in Corsica]." On April 16, 1795: "The attempt of the enemy will be against Italy." Again, on October 27, while commanding a light squadron off the Genoese Riviera to cover the left flank of our Austrian Allies: "My situation with this army has convinced me . . . of the futility of continental alliances."

At that time a far more energetic commander, Jervis, was on his way to take command of the Mediterranean fleet; and Nelson, noting the change, writes with more hopeful insistence as to the need of re-occupying Vado Bay and helping the Austro - Sardinian defenders of the pass above named: "If they (the French) mean to carry on the war, they must penetrate into Italy. Holland and Flanders, with their own country, they have stripped. Italy is the gold-mine, and, if once entered, is without the means of resistance." Eyes as keen as his had already discerned the same truth; and a will still more masterful was preparing to deal the fatal blow to old Europe at the then vital spot, the pass north-west of Savona. Had our Allies acted with a tithe of the energy and skill of either Bonaparte or Nelson, Italy need not have been lost. As is well known, their co-operation was imperfect and tardy, but through no fault of Nelson. He with his squadron hovered off that coast, harassing the French flank and stopping their sea-borne supplies. On April 12 (the very day on which Bonaparte dealt his first sudden blows at the Allies' joint) he had an interview with the Austrian *aide-de-camp*, and offered once more to help at any point of the coast to which the Allies should penetrate. At that very time Bonaparte was driving the Austrian vanguard inland, and in the following days Nelson's worst fears were realised, so that on May 16 he wrote : " I very much fear that England, who commenced the war with all Europe for her Allies, will finish it by having nearly all Europe for her enemies "—a correct horoscope of the situation in 1801.

As Nelson expected, Spain soon declared war. Thereupon he expressed the confident hope of beating with 22 sail the Franco-Spanish fleet of 35 or more, adding that Jervis by his superior skill would almost certainly be able on some occasion to attack part of that large array when separated or becalmed. What a remarkable forecast of what happened off St. Vincent on St. Valentine's day, 1797 ! Jervis seized exactly such an opportunity, and Nelson clinched it, the result being that 15 decisively beat 27.

The notion still persists that Nelson won his victories by " going straight at 'em." It is therefore desirable to note that his quick and incisive attacks were the result of long and careful study of all likely contingencies, such as his nimble imagination enabled him to picture. Thus, during the long and weary chase of Bonaparte's oriental Armada in June–July 1798, he summoned his captains on board the " Vanguard " on favourable occasions (so Captain Sir Edward Berry states) to discuss and explain his plans for assailing the enemy—" whatever their situation or position might be, by day or night. There was no possible position in which they could be found that he did not take into his calculation, and for the most advantageous attack." Consequently, after sighting the French fleet at anchor in Aboukir Bay, he signalled " that it was his intention to attack the enemy's van and centre as they lay at anchor and according to the plan before developed."

The victory was due largely to the surprise attack ; but it was no surprise for his " band of brothers," who, one and all, sailed in with swift comprehension of their commander's design, because he had had the foresight to outline the situation which then materialised.  How different from Rodney, whose novel design of concentrating on the hostile rear off Martinique on April 17, 1780, miscarried because he lacked the sympathetic foresight to picture their bewilderment at this change of tactics.

Early in the long chase after Bonaparte's force, Nelson surmised that the ultimate aim of the French was to co-operate with Tippoo Sultan and expel us from India. Therefore, while collecting the prizes in Aboukir Bay, he despatched Lieut. Duval of H.M.S. "Zealous" to Bombay, *via* Alexandretta and Basra, to warn the Governor-General at Calcutta of this design ; and his sagacious measure led to the adoption of plans which brought about the fall of Tippoo at Seringapatam in the following spring.

In other respects Nelson's faculties shone with a more fitful radiance after his triumph at the Nile.  The painful scalp wound perhaps accounts for this temporary falling off, which led him to picture the French entirely cut off and almost starving in Egypt, and the Austrians forthwith recovering Italy.  His extremely sanguine outlook was soon to be strengthened by contact with the Hamiltons at Naples.  These ominous phrases occur in his letter of October 4 to St. Vincent : " I am writing opposite Lady Hamilton, therefore you will not be surprised at the glorious jumble of this letter ; . . . our hearts and hands must be all in a flutter ; Naples is a dangerous place."  Though resisting for a time this flood of infatuation, he began to lose both his mental and moral balance, the result being his unwise advice to the Neapolitan Court forthwith to attack France (" boldest measures are the safest ").  The partial " Sicilianising " of his political outlook may also account for the odd statements as to the valuelessness of Malta for us, and the propriety of its reversion to the King of Naples.  Even down to the parliamentary debates of

1801–02 on the peace, he maintained the same thesis, always defending Addington's intended retrocession of that island to the Knights of St. John.   His pronouncements on this topic were the more singular because that complaisant Premier was surrendering Minorca to Spain, thus leaving us without a single naval base east of Gibraltar.   The speedy resumption of Oriental designs by Napoleon and the consequent rupture with England opened Nelson's eyes, and led to the final verdict that Malta was " a most important outwork to India."

As Nelson's foresight was often at fault in the years 1799–1802, the question arises whether that valuable quality is not the efflorescence of all the powers of the mind acting in complete harmony.   Any disproportion between them, any jarring of passion or remorse, mars their smooth working and produces opinions more or less distorted.   The phrase in Nelson's letter cited above as to the glorious jumble of his thoughts when that erotic passion first stole upon him is highly significant; and it cannot be a fortuitous coincidence that these years, which witnessed the climax of that passion, were marked also by a temporary decline of his mental faculties and of his efficiency as Admiral.

From this statement we must, however, except the Copenhagen campaign.   England's ringing call to action early in 1801 at the crisis of the Armed Neutrality League once more braced his powers.   In that springtide he wrote : " We have the dominion of the Seas and all the devils in hell cannot take it from us if our wooden walls have fair play."   Also, on March 24, to his rather leisurely commander-in-chief, Sir Hyde Parker : " Not a moment should be lost in attacking the enemy ; they will every day and hour be stronger ; we never shall be so good a match for them as at this moment. . . . Never did our country depend so much on the success of any fleet as on this." Having by marvellous foresight, winged with audacity, forced the Danes to an armistice at Copenhagen, he was for speeding on to Reval and Cronstadt to cow the arch-enemy

Russia, by catching her fleets icebound in those ports.   But for delays and the change of ruler at Petersburg he might have achieved much in the Gulf of Finland ; for he always aimed at sparing the Danes and bringing to book the mad Czar Paul, the contriver of the League.

Thus amidst the grave perils of that springtide Nelson found himself once more.   In no part of his career did he evince a more complete union of daring with far-seeing prudence than in the Baltic campaign.   How to explain this glorious rally after the drop of the previous years is a mystery ; for Colonel Stewart, who sailed with him in the " Elephant," recorded that he was ever ill.at ease.   Perhaps danger and the load of responsibility deadened the moral disquiet within.   To no crisis of his life are the eloquent words of Vice-Admiral Colomb more applicable : " His excitement never carried him away, his judgment let his excitement share alike with itself ; and the two worked together in producing acts which the coolest criticism of after years only succeeds in commending as at once the simplest and the wisest.   Nelson in action with an opposing fleet stands more nearly as a specially inspired being than any great man of modern times." [1]   To this eulogy I may venture to add as supplement that Nelson, while coolly facing all present perils, ever kept his mind alert as to future contingencies.   After settling with the Danish Crown the plan of the Armistice, his alert mind grasped at another boon : " Now, Sir, this is settled ; suppose we write Peace instead of Armistice."

On his return to home waters to lay the spectre of a French invasion he longs " to catch that Bonaparte on the water," and so end the war ; but, alas, the First Consul only says to his seamen " Allez-vous-en," and not " Allons, mes amis."   Though impressed at first by the imposing apparatus of the French and Dutch flotillas, Nelson soon discerns the hollowness of the menace, except perhaps from the Scheldt against our East coast.   And in September 1801 he thus sums up : " This boat-business must be over : it

[1] " From Howard to Nelson," p. 453.

may be a part of a great plan of invasion, but can never be
the only one "—the very conclusion at which Napoleon
arrived in 1804, after prolonged and costly preparations for
the passage of the strait by his flotilla without a convoying
fleet.

" Is it Ireland or Egypt ? " was the question agitating
Nelson's brain during his distant blockade of the Toulon
fleet in 1803–05.  Possibly, as Colomb states, he assigned
too great importance to the alternative that Napoleon would
again seize Egypt ;  but, as commander of our Mediterranean
fleet, he had to protect the Levantine trade ;  and Napoleon's
preparations, framed with marvellous cunning, seemed to
point eastwards.  As Nelson said, all was conjecture until
the Frenchmen's course was credibly reported ;  and his
outlook frigate, " Active," reported that their fleet might
be making for the East.  Thither Nelson proceeded, but in
vain.  All the more remarkable, then, is his subsequent
chase after the combined fleet to the West Indies.  The
positive evidence as to that course was so slight that
nobody but Nelson would have dared to risk a fiasco in
that quarter such as befell Calder in 1799.  When nearing
Madeira he wrote (May 14, 1805) : " Under the most
serious consideration which I can give from all I hear, I
rather think that the West Indies must be the destination
of the combined squadrons."  This time he was right ;
and, not long after, he thus avowed to a Jamaican a further
reason for chasing thither : " I was bred, as you know, in
the good old school, and taught to appreciate the value of
our West India possessions."  Thus the snippets of nautical
evidence picked up off Cape St. Vincent, reinforced by his
early love of the West Indies, sent him speeding to Barbados.  A brilliant conjecture !  But, with England in
danger from the Brest fleet, a flotilla far greater than in
1801, and Napoleon's Grand Army ready at Boulogne, how
hazardous a conjecture !  Almost equally remarkable was
his resolve, when off Grenada and Montserrat, to head back
to Europe.  A perusal of these hundreds of anxious letters
enforces a truth often forgotten, that, at bottom, war is an

affair of getting news, interpreting it, and acting upon it. As he himself wrote when beset by the fog of war : " In sea affairs nothing is impossible, and nothing improbable."[1]

At Trafalgar, as at the Nile, the unswerving onset was the outcome, not of mere hardihood as is often supposed, but of carefully-thought-out plans.  Nelson gleaned much from the tactics employed by Rodney in April 1782, by Howe on June 1, 1794, and by Duncan at Camperdown. But, as usual, he looked forward to the probable contingencies.  The first outline of the Trafalgar plan appears to have been sketched during the long chase to the West Indies and back.  The second and more definite programme was penned off Cadiz, twelve days before the battle, and was explained to his captains with the proviso : " Something must be left to chance : nothing is sure in a sea-fight beyond all others."  But the great leader indicated the general line of action, leaving to Collingwood much liberty in regard to details.  Thus, as at the Nile, few signals were necessary.  He had indicated the guiding principle of the attack ; and, by a last flash of that almost uncanny prescience, he exclaimed to Captain Blackwood of the " Euryalus " frigate, as they bore down on the hostile line, " God bless you, Blackwood ; I shall never speak to you again."

[1] Nicolas, vi. 133.

# VIII

## THE STATE OF NELSON'S FLEET BEFORE TRAFALGAR

THE condition of a fleet after long and trying services is often a test of the care and foresight of the commander-in-chief; and rarely were these qualities more needed than in the case of the Mediterranean squadron during the years 1803–05. Nelson's difficulties in keeping his ships, while off Toulon, in efficient condition and their crews in good health are too well known to need recounting here. During twenty-two months he observed Toulon; and at the end of that time, in spite of insufficient reliefs and the great difficulty of procuring fresh meat, water and vegetables, his ships were able to pursue Villeneuve and Gravina to the West Indies and back without having the ships (except the old " Superb ") unseaworthy or their crews decimated by scurvy. The miracle of the " Superb " keeping up with the fleet was equalled by the extraordinary healthiness of the crews. Nelson was only nine days looking round the Leeward Islands, and therefore had very little time to refresh the men or lay in a sufficient store of necessaries. He left St. John's Road, Antigua, on June 13, 1805, and anchored at Gibraltar on July 19. There he set foot on shore for the first time since June 16, 1803, not having left the " Victory " in the interval. On the next day the fleet proceeded to Tetuan Bay for supplies of fresh water and bullocks. Thence, in pursuance of orders, he proceeded northwards to join Admiral Cornwallis off Ushant, as he did on August 15; and leaving nine sail with him, made sail with the "Victory" and "Superb" for Spithead, which he reached on the 18th. The condition of his ships after so prolonged and exhausting a term of service is of so much interest that it may be well to publish the following official accounts:

## LIST OF LORD NELSON'S SHIPS ON AUGUST 15, 1805.

| Ships. | Captains. | Provisions. | Stores. | Health. | Remarks. |
|---|---|---|---|---|---|
| VICTORY . | T. M. Hardy | Three months | Completed for Channel service July 22 last | Little scurvy | Requires to be looked at before winter |
| CANOPUS . | T. W. Austen | do. | do. | do. | Requires to be docked before winter |
| SUPERB . | R. G. Keats | One month | One month | do. | Greatly in need of docking and new foremast |
| SPENCER . | Hon. R. R. Stopford | Three months | Three months | do. | Fit for service |
| BELLEISLE . | W. Hargood | do. | do. | Much scurvy | Requires to be docked before winter |
| SPARTIATE . | Sir F. Laforey | do. | do. | Little scurvy | Has been on shore and needs looking at |
| CONQUEROR . | J. Pellew | do. | do. | do. | Fit for service |
| TIGRE . | B. Hallowell | do. | do. | do. | do. |
| LEVIATHAN . | H. W. Bayntum | do. | do. | do. | do. |
| DONEGAL . | P. Malcolm | do. | do. | do. | Requires docking before winter |
| SWIFTSURE . | W. G. Rutherford | do. | do. | do. | Fit for service |

To Hon. WILLIAM CORNWALLIS,  
    Admiral of the White,  
        Commander-in-Chief.

(Signed)  NELSON AND BRONTE.

In a Report to Nelson, dated H.M.S. " Victory " at Spithead, August 18, 1805, the physician of the fleet, Leonard Gillespie, certified the number of sick on each ship as follows: "Victory," 14; "Canopus," 36; "Superb," 20; "Spencer," 15; "Swiftsure," 29; "Belleisle," 15; "Conqueror," 10; "Tigre," 11; "Leviathan," 26; "Donegal," 19. He reports the total number of deaths in the fleet from August 13, 1803, to August 4, 1805, as 110, and the cases sent to hospital as 141. He appends the following observations, which may be quoted in full. (It should be understood that the term " scorbutics " applies to men in a scorbutic condition, though not suffering from scurvy):

" Of these there were then (August 4, 1805) only 23 cases of scurvy, 10 fever, 9 fluxes, 32 ulcers, 45 wounds and accidents, 10 rheumatism, 23 'Pulmonic Inflammations'; 2 venereal (both on the 'Donegal'); other complaints, 60; confined to bed, 7. The 'Spencer' and 'Tigre' have 40 scorbutics each; 'Belleisle' 160 scorbutics; 'Conqueror' 36 scorbutics. The number of scorbutics has considerably decreased in the Fleet, in consequence of the refreshments procured at Tetuan and Gibraltar. The pleasing and exhilarating prospect of soon seeing England may have been attended with the most happy effects amongst the ships' companies in checking the progress of the scurvy, a disease which is very much influenced by the passions of the mind, and which has been observed to spread itself as if by contagion under the influence of the depressing passions amongst bodies of men. Altho' 23 men only are deemed unfit for duty on account of scurvy, yet there is every reason to suppose that almost all the sick in the Fleet are more or less scorbutic, as scurvy often becomes complicated with a variety of different diseases, rendering their cure difficult or impossible without the aid of anti-scorbutics. It would also appear that a very large pro-portion of the men composing the ships' companies of the Fleet are more or less scorbutic in habit of body and stand in need of the salutary aid of vegetables and fresh meat in order to re-establish a vigorous state of health for the time and guard them for some time to come against the conse-quence of scorbutic habit."

After presenting an abstract of the totals of deaths and sick, Gillespie continues :

" The above statement exhibits the most convincing and satisfactory proofs of the advantages arising from the practice of the improvements adopted in this Fleet for the purpose of preserving the crews in good health and the ships wholesome ; and if compared with the accounts of the state of health of Fleets or Squadrons on foreign Stations in former wars, the result will be found to show the importance of the regulations now used in preserving the lives and health of British seamen. Thus we find Dr. Blane, Physician to the Fleet in the West Indies in the year 1781, in a memorial presented by him in October of that year to the Lords of the Admiralty on the health of seamen, deploring the rapid expenditure of seamen in the navy and stating that during one year in a fleet of 20 sail of the line, manned by 12,000 seamen, there died on board 715 men and in the hospitals 862 men, forming a total of 1577 men, of which number only 59 died in consequence of wounds ; during the same period 350 men were invalided. The above shows that one man in seven died in the course of one year in the said Fleet.

" The following causes may be assigned for the high state of health in which the Fleet under the command of Lord Nelson has been preserved for upward of two years, unexampled perhaps in any fleet or squadron heretofore employed on a foreign station.   (I.) The attention paid by His Lordship to the victualling and purveying for the Fleet, in causing good wholesome wine to be used in room of spirits ; fresh beef as often as it could possibly be procured. Vegetables and fruit were always provided in sufficient quantity when they could be purchased, and an abundant supply of excellent sweet water was always allowed to the ships' companies.   (II.) The ships were preserved as free as possible from the baneful effects of humidity, by avoiding the wetting the decks (at least between the decks) and by the use of stoves and ventilation below.   (III.) The constant activity and motion in which the Fleet was preserved, being always at sea and never exposed to the consequences of the idleness and intemperance which too often take place on board ships lying in harbour, may doubtless be assigned as a principal cause of the good state of health of the crews of this fleet.   (IV.) Intemperance and skulking were never, perhaps, so little practised in any fleet as in this.   As ships were never in port, the opportunity of procuring spirits, or of going to a Hospital by imposing on the Surgeons were (*sic*) difficult or impossible :  hence these causes of disease were subtracted. (V.) The promoting cheerfulness amongst the men was encouraged by music, dancing and theatrical amusements ;  the example of which was given by the Commander-in-Chief in the 'Victory' and may with reason be reckoned amongst the causes of the preservation of the health of the men.   (VI.) The sick were, in general, very comfortably accommodated, lodged in airy sick-berths, in many ships placed on a regular sick-diet, and supplied with live stock, vegetables, fruit, soft bread, macaroni and other articles of diet and refreshments whenever the circumstances of the service would admit of these supplies being furnished.   (VII.) By a standing order of the Commander-in-Chief Peruvian Bark mixed in wine or spirits was regularly served to the men employed on the service of wooding and watering ;  a dram of Peruvian Bark to one gill of spirits or two gills of wine was the proportion allowed for each man, to be given to the men on going on shore and after returning on board. . . . It is well known to experienced officers in the Navy that on foreign stations sickness very often finds its entrance into ships of war from the wooding and watering parties being first attacked by fevers in consequence of fatigue and exposure, which fevers very often spread among the ships' company and become a formidable and epidemic disease.

                    " (Signed) LEONARD GILLESPIE,
                              Physician to the Fleet.

" ' Victory', at Sea, August 14, 1805."


    The extreme importance of the health of a fleet is seen if we contrast the deplorable wastage in Rodney's crews in the West Indies in 1781 with that of Nelson's crews in 1803–05.   In the former fleet (of course, on an unhealthy station) 1516 men died of sickness, exclusive of wounds, in a single year, out of a total of about 12,000 men. On Nelson's eleven ships, carrying about 6500 men, the

total number of deaths was 110, and only 141 men were
sent to hospital in a period of two years, less nine days.
Therefore, in spite of the exceptionally long and trying
service off Toulon and the chase to the West Indies and
back, Nelson's crews had suffered practically no diminution
of strength.

The topic of vital statistics of the Royal Navy has
received far too little attention ; for it is fairly certain that
when, in the old days, a fleet, or certain units of it, behaved
badly, sickness was as often as not the cause.   Scurvy seems
to have been specially rife in British ships, especially those
on distant stations, because of the insistence of the men on
a meat diet, which of course meant salt meat.   French
and, still more, Spanish fleets were a prey to more violent
epidemics, probably because of the lower standard of
cleanliness maintained on board.   The fiasco of the
Franco-Spanish attempt on Plymouth in 1779 is explicable,
partly at least, by the outbreak on board the Spanish ships
of a plague which finally put out of action that imposing
Armada.   There is also an illuminating sentence in Nelson's
letter of July 14, 1793.   After noting that Lord Hood's
fleet off Ivica had spoken with the Allied Spanish fleet,
which was returning to port crowded with sick, he writes :
" The captain of the [Spanish] frigate said, ' It was no
wonder they were sickly, for they had been sixty days at
sea.' "   Nelson adds that by then a British crew would be
in fine condition.[1]

Throughout his despatches there appears the conviction
that British crews far surpass those of France or Spain ;
and this belief is founded on their superior healthiness.
Take his last voyage, that of 1805.   Several times he writes
that the hostile crews are very sickly, while his are in good
condition ;  and on August 18, 1805, at Spithead, he refers
to those of the " Victory " and " Superb " as being in
perfect health.[2]

Whether the Franco-Spanish fleet, on its return to

[1] Nicolas, " Despatches . . . of Nelson," i. p. 312.
[2] *Ibid.* vii. p. 8.

home waters, was as sickly as believed, Nelson is open to question ; for the evidence is conflicting. Two reports, after Calder's action of July 22, stated that there was much illness aboard, but another denied it, and hazarded the assertion that the Spanish ships were free from disease.[1] This last is incredible ; and it is in flat contradiction to Villeneuve's report after the battle of July 22, which ran : " . . . les malades augmentaient dans toute l'escadre . . . il me devenait indispensable de toucher dans quelque port pour y débarquer les malades et les blessés qui encombraient les vaisseaux." [2]

As to Nelson's care in providing his men with fresh water, fresh meat, and vegetables, his despatches bear witness to the very end. On October 3, 1805, he expressed his resolve to compel the neutral Portuguese to allow his boats to procure fresh water, even if such a step led to diplomatic protests. It is also not too much to say that his prolonged observation of Toulon was rendered possible only by his extreme care in procuring refreshments for the crews. Thus, twice over he ordered twenty tons of onions, and on one occasion 30,000 oranges.[3] Judging from the above-cited reports, Gillespie brought equal zeal and intelligence to his duties. There is also good evidence that the health of the crews had of late received due attention from the Admiralty. In and after 1795 lime-juice was regularly served to ships commissioned for distant stations. That anti-scorbutic had long been used in East Indiamen ; but its issue to the Navy was due to the efforts of Drs. Blane and Harness. Besides Nelson, other Admirals also bestowed great care on the health of their crews. In this brief survey I need merely mention Collingwood, who, during the blockade of Cadiz in the winter of 1797–8, wrote that he kept his wits at work how to amuse his men so as to maintain their health. "Every moonlight night the sailors dance ; and there seems as much mirth and festivity as if

---

[1] J. Leyland, "Blockade of Brest" (1803-1805), ii. pp. 319, 324.
[2] E. Desbrière, "La Campagne maritime de 1805," p. 68.
[3] Nicolas, v. 303, 352, 432, 474, etc.

we were in Wapping itself."[1]  Such were the Admirals who prepared their men for the final test.  At Trafalgar British gunnery was thrice as effective as that of the combined fleet.  But gunnery depends very largely on the condition of the man behind the gun.

[1] " Correspondence of Collingwood," p. 64.

## IX

## THE BRITISH TITLE TO MALTA

DISCUSSION of this topic may perhaps seem superfluous. But it does not seem so to certain circles in
Malta and Italy. It may therefore be well to examine their
statements and to bring them to the test of fact.

Curiously enough, the first vocal Maltese malcontent
was a discredited English official, William Eton, who, after
holding a subordinate post in that island and becoming
suspect to the British authorities, returned to England in
the autumn of 1802 and forthwith wrote a book entitled
"Materials for an authentic History of Malta." When
published finally in 1807, it was found to contain a sharp
attack on Captain Sir Alexander Ball, formerly of H.M.S.
"Alexander," who had held together the native Maltese
levies during the two years' siege of the French garrison in
Valetta (1798–1800). Eton charged Ball with tyrannical
acts, especially the abolition of the local *Consiglio Popolare*,
which he (Eton) styled a Parliament. Ball rebutted the
charge by proving that when he took command of the
Maltese levies they were rent by schisms and factions
ruinous both to civil order and military discipline. Of his
own accord he suggested a Congress of the Notables for the
restoration of order, and received much help from that body.
It was a military measure which naturally ceased with the
capitulation of the French garrison in September 1800. A
Maltese gentleman, Sir Ferdinand Inglott, also proved that
the *Consiglio* had no legislative powers ; and the French

historian Miège [1] admitted that the Maltese had no notion of representative institutions.

In the same year in which Eton's book saw the light an Irishman named Dillon repeated Eton's charges and added one of his own, viz. : that " The French garrison was driven by the Maltese within the lines of the fortifications [of Valetta] and would have had to surrender to the Maltese if the combined [Franco-Spanish] fleet had not appeared, or if they had delayed their arrival." This theme, as to the predominant part played by the Maltese during the siege of 1798–1800, was embroidered on by the Marchese Testaferrata, who, in a letter of January 1812 to Earl Bathurst, sought to magnify their achievements and belittle those of the British squadron and troops. He added that during fifteen months the struggle was carried on solely at the expense of the Maltese, that during the siege of Valetta they lost " by sickness and the sword of the enemy about 20,000 persons, while *our* handful of auxiliaries lost not one soldier killed by the enemy " ; also that finally the English secretly granted a capitulation to the French.

In that year also Monsignor Bres stated in writing to the British Commissioners that " nobody can have the impudence to deny that the Maltese alone by their own efforts broke the French thraldom," and, aided by their auxiliaries (English, Portuguese and Sicilians), " drove the French out of the principal fortifications of Malta." In 1839 Baron de Piro published a book, " Squarci di Storia," in which he asserted that the native Maltese were deeply attached to the rule of the Knights of St. John (which fell at Bonaparte's touch in 1798) ; also that in the autumn of 1798 " the English commanders, military and naval, found themselves at the head of an armed and victorious people, provided with every need as to munitions of war and food." Finally he repeated the story as to our gratuitously granting a capitulation to the French, thereby shamefully bartering away the blood of 20,000 Maltese. Finally, in 1843, Baron

[1] Miège, " Histoire de Malte," 1840, iii. ch. 11. See, too, Hardman, " Hist. of Malta," ch. 23.

Azopardi declared in his "Annals of Malta" that the Maltese in 1802 made a voluntary donation of the island to Great Britain.

These statements have been tricked out by various writers up to comparatively recent times, in spite of their skilful refutation by Dr. Augusto Bartolo in a series of letters brought together in his work "The Sovereignty of Malta" (Malta, "Daily Malta Chronicle" Office, 1909). In that year also appeared "A History of Malta" (1798–1815), by the late Mr. William Hardman of Valetta, which I edited, with introduction and notes. As this volume was too bulky and crowded with documents to attract much attention, and has long been out of print, it may be worth while to review the evidence on the questions in dispute, which unfortunately are still often raked up.

In proof of the hatred of the Maltese for the rule of the Knights of St. John, which was then at its worst, I may quote the testimony of Mr. Williams, British Consul at Valetta, on June 30, 1798, that Bonaparte before his attack on that city, knew there were quite 4000 native Maltese in his favour; and he adds, "I do believe the Maltese (*sic*) have given the island to the French to get rid of the Knights." [1] Certainly the feuds between the Knights and the natives paralysed the half-hearted defence, especially in Cottonera and at the Knights' Tower, where the populace rose against the Order and killed or imprisoned several of its members. The householders also assembled and drew up a demand for surrender, to which the Grand Master, Hompesch, was forced to assent. These facts speak for themselves.

The next question in dispute turns on the burdens borne respectively by the British and Maltese during the two years' siege of the French garrison in Valetta. That the natives did well in spite of great difficulties is admitted by all British officers and writers; but the version presented by Testaferrata, Bres, and de Piro, is at least greatly

[1] Foreign Office Archives, Malta, No. 1. See, too, Miège, "Hist. de Malte," ch. 11.

exaggerated ; for they almost entirely ignore the decisive
part which sea power played in the reduction of Valetta.
In this connection the following facts are highly significant :
(1) The native Maltese did not rise against the French troops
until September 2, 1798, that is, five days after the arrival
of the French warship " Guillaume Tell " at Valetta
bringing news of the disaster at the Nile.  Previous anti-
clerical actions of the French had led to no rising : that
of September 2 was clearly prompted by knowledge that
the French had lost command of the Mediterranean.  The
French commander, General Vaubois, now brought all his
troops into Valetta.  (2) On September 25 Captain Saumarez in H.M.S. " Orion," with six more sail, convoying
the French prizes from the Nile to Gibraltar, hove-to off
Malta and supplied to the local levies 1062 muskets, 20,740
ball cartridges, etc.  Previously they had only 800 muskets,
mostly shot-guns.[1]  (3) The inhabitants were then being
helped by a Portuguese squadron under de Niza, and were
about to be aided by Nelson after October 24.  He then
found that the King of Naples, whom he hastily assumed
to be the present owner of Malta, had sent no food or arms
to help the natives.  These, on October 25, complained to
Nelson of their " extreme penury of munitions of war,"
and of food : they had only 35 iron cannon and no mortars.
The French had 552 cannon and 58 mortars.  (4) As to
food supplies, General Vaubois, while withdrawing his out-
posts, had swept all corn, etc. into Valetta, the consequence
being terrible scarcity outside ; for the island normally
produced corn enough to feed the people during only four
months out of the twelve.  Sir William Hamilton, British
Ambassador at Naples, writing on November 6, 1798 to
Lord Grenville, stated that, but for our supplies of food
and arms, the natives must have submitted to the French.
Vaubois increased the food crisis by expelling 10,000 people
from Valetta.  Writing to the Directory at Paris he added :
" *Des vivres, et Malte sera pour toujours à la République.*" [2]

[1] Hardman, " Hist. of Malta," p. 110 ; Miège, iii. 205.
[2] Hardman, 126-143.

Thus within and without of Valetta it was seen that the issue of the siege turned essentially on food.

Other facts relevant to the dispute are these : Captain Ball, R.N., after helping to reduce the French garrison of Gozo, became practically the leader of the Maltese levies ; he soon gained their confidence and stilled the jealous quarrels of their chiefs. His plan of storming the Cottonera fortifications in mid-January 1799 failed owing to the backwardness, not to say cowardice, of the Maltese, who had been discouraged by the failure of a plot inside Valetta. On January 26 their leaders wrote to Nelson stating that the British and Portuguese warships had "guarded the safety and liberty of this people," but they received no help from Naples. " Our desolation is complete and the urgency is inexpressible. Our enemies, enclosed within the impregnable fortifications, the work of two centuries, obstinately resist ; and they are in possession of wheat which will last a long time." This last was due to a French brig slipping by night into Valetta (January 13), bringing enough food for the whole summer, so Vaubois reported.[1] So much for the assertion that the English found themselves at the head of " an armed and victorious people," provided with plenty of food and munitions. On the contrary, Vaubois assured the French Directory on April 1, 1799 of his great satisfaction that the Maltese had revolted, otherwise he would have had to feed nearly 100,000 people, which would quickly have emptied his stores during the British naval blockade.[2]

There is a half truth in Dillon's statement, quoted above, as to the possibility of the French surrendering in May 1799 but for the arrival of Bruix's Franco-Spanish fleet in the Mediterranean. But Dillon ignored the arrival of food for the Valetta garrison by that French brig, also the far more important fact that the incursion of Bruix, and the consequent withdrawal of all the British warships for the purpose of effecting a concentration, prove that the fate of Malta depended entirely on sea power. Our vessels had

[1] Hardman, 164-169.  [2] *Ibid.* 606.

to leave Valetta unwatched during six weeks, within which time Vaubois had command of Maltese waters and swept in much food by coasting vessels. But he never attempted to overpower the native levies (then in great distress and disorder) and the small British force which had been landed to help them, because his garrison was semi-mutinous and he could not afford to leave any part of the immense *enceinte* unguarded. His men eagerly awaited the approach of Bruix, who, however, soon left the Mediterranean. This interlude of six weeks showed conclusively that the maritime blockade of Valetta alone counted for anything.[1]

At that time the position of the Maltese was desperate. Ball wrote to Nelson on April 12, 1799, " They are so reduced by sickness and disheartened for want of pay, clothes, and nourishment that it is with the utmost difficulty that I can rally them and keep them at their posts." He begged Nelson to send £5000 from Palermo at once for the purchase of food. The Sicilian Government despatched £3500. During Ball's temporary absence, his lieutenant, Vivion, reported (June 25) that the Maltese would not obey their own chiefs but only British officers.[2]

It is now time to consider the claims of the extreme Italian section that Malta belonged of right to the King of Naples. Undoubtedly, they possess some historic basis ; for since the time of the Norman conquest of Sicily Malta had been under the suzerainty of the King of that island. That tie had, however, weakened with age, especially after the year 1530, when Malta was granted in perpetual gift to the Knights of St. John by the Emperor Charles V. In 1798 it was little more than a traditional tie. After the rising of September 2 against the French, Canon Caruana, the chief representative of the Maltese, urged them " to place themselves under the protection of the King of Sicily, proclaiming him as their sovereign "— a form of words which implies that the Sicilian suzerainty

[1] *Ibid.* 212-218, 589.     [2] *Ibid.* 210-215.

had lapsed.  The Maltese now implored his protection as their sovereign.  But, his help being tardy and utterly inadequate (he was a fugitive from Naples at Palermo in the first half of 1799), their Sicilian ardour soon cooled. On March 31, 1799 the Maltese Congress unanimously begged Nelson to forward to George III. their urgent petition to have him as king, " under whose incorruptible and mild government all his subjects live happily."  They also begged Ferdinand of Naples to allow his sovereignty to be transferred to George III.[1]  Their anxiety on this head was increased by the report that Russian troops were coming to capture Valetta and claim the islands for the Czar Paul, who, as Grand Master of the Order of St. John, would be certain to restore the rule of the Knights, supported by Russian bayonets.  British sovereignty was therefore hailed as the best solution of the dispute as to the lordship of Malta.  Ferdinand and Maria Carolina of Naples of course eagerly welcomed their new sovereignty (as also did Nelson), but clearly it amounted to very little ; and that little was dissipated by their slackness and the corruption of their underlings.

By July 9, 1799 the Pitt Ministry had decided that Malta must revert to the Knights of St. John, "who acknowledged the Emperor of Russia as Grand Master." [2] At that time Grenville was anxious to strengthen the new Anglo-Russian alliance in order to expel the French from Italy and Germany ; and George III. and he seem to have ignored the Maltese offer of sovereignty to Great Britain. To restore the island to its lawful owners, the Knights, satisfied both the claims of legitimacy and the dictates of diplomacy, Paul being crazily eager to possess the island hallowed by association with his namesake.  From the recently published " Spencer Papers " (III., p. 103) it is clear that the Earl, then First Lord of the Admiralty, urgently warned Nelson to do nothing which might arouse the jealousy of that irascible potentate, who, if he had proved constant, and had sent troops to help

---

[1] Hardman, 203-205.          [2] *Ibid.* 218.

in the siege, would certainly have become sovereign of Malta.

As Paul disappointed all hopes and soon turned savagely against England, this solution of the Maltese problem vanished into air. Not a Russian ship or battalion appeared on the scene; and not until February 1800 did 1600 Neapolitan troops arrive and help to complete the line of investment.[1] Nelson's letters throw light on the situation. He now regarded the Order of St. John as the legal successor to the French, and the King of Naples as only " founder-lord." As to the besiegers of Valetta, he reckons that the British troops will exceed 2500; and there are always 500 seamen ashore, while "the Maltese in arms, volunteers, never exceed 3000." He has helped to feed 60,000 Maltese, whose schisms and quarrels have necessitated the appointment of Captain Ball to command. The expenses of the British blockading squadron off Valetta have been fully £180,000.[2]

Help was then expected from General Graham's garrison at Messina; and his adjutant, Lindenthal, who was sent on in advance to report, expressed surprise on December 6, 1799 that the French did not attack the relatively feeble besiegers, who consisted of 800 British soldiers, 400 marines, and 1500 Maltese soldiers, besides 1000 more armed Maltese. As to the Maltese, he said—" they are very much attached to us and have done wonders." The arrival of Graham's force on December 11 lessened the dangers of the besiegers on land. He found that 2358 Maltese were under arms and deemed their position very precarious if Vaubois should attack. The chief difficulty, however, through that winter was to keep the Maltese alive. Rear-Admiral Troubridge worked hard to extort food supplies from the Sicilian officials, who dishonestly withheld them or diverted them elsewhere. In January 1800 he reported that the famishing Maltese were seizing our soldiers' rations. Only by his exertions and those of Nelson and Ball was a serious crisis averted.

---

[1] *Ibid.* 297.
[2] Nicolas, " Despatches of Nelson," iv. 75-79.

Inside Valetta the French were little better off.  Vaubois then had only 2200 effectives, who, being closely rationed, were weak and discontented.  These facts explain his not attacking the besiegers.  A sortie would denude his extensive works and expose Fort Ricasoli, at the mouth of the harbour, to a joint onset by the blockading ships and troops.[1]  Besides, how would the French benefit by a victory on land which would merely burden them with prisoners to feed ?  His only hope was the arrival of a French squadron from Toulon ; and deep was his despair on hearing of the destruction of that of Admiral Perrée on February 18, 1800.  He therefore determined to send off the " Guillaume Tell " so as to lessen the number of mouths to feed.[2]  She was captured ; but this step and the arrival of the " Bellona " and " Marguérite " from France enabled him to hold out until early in September.

In spite of the arrival in June of 1500 British troops from the Minorca garrison, Graham's successor, General Pigot, decided, and surely with reason, not to assault the vast fortifications of Valetta.  Hunger was there doing its work far more surely, so that on August 7 he expected the surrender within about six weeks.[3]  Vaubois could calculate that date more nearly.  By August 3 his garrison had only meagre rations of bread, which he reckoned would last until September 2.  Actually he held out until September 4, and at the time of his surrender the fortress was intact.  On both sides, then, the issue turned on food.  Thanks to the British squadron, the Maltese survived the previous terrible winter, and the same invisible agency assured the capitulation of Valetta, which was the logical outcome of Nelson's victory at the Nile.

As to the proportion of casualties among the besiegers, Ball reported officially on March 6, 1801 that the Maltese had lost altogether three hundred killed and wounded.[4]

[1] Hardman, 235-259, 623-627
[2] *Ibid.* 629-631.
[3] *Ibid.* 306-310, 638-641.
[4] Colonial Office Records, Malta, No. 2.

The number of British casualties on shore is not known.
Probably it was small; for both Graham and Pigot disapproved of assaults on an impregnable fortress; but it
is known that of the 400 or 500 British marines serving on
the island all but 178 were in July 1800 ill with Maltese
fever,[1] and probably all our troops landed there lost heavily
from that cause. As we have seen, the Marchese Testaferrata
gave out that his people lost 20,000 "by sickness and the sword
of the enemy," and that our troops lost not one man killed.
Both assertions are wildly false; for the British held the
front line during most of the siege. He also ignored the
British casualties incurred during the sea blockade, though
it was far more effective in assuring the surrender of Valetta
than were the puny efforts on land against its impregnable
ramparts. It is known that the British casualties in the
fights with the " Généreux " and the " Guillaume Tell "
amounted to 136 killed and wounded.[2]

In the matter of expense, the British Government bore
the chief part in saving the Maltese from starvation. The
Neapolitan Government acted tardily, its officials dishonestly, with respect to food supplies, which accounts for
the dislike of it manifested by the islanders. Ball was
annoyed when (as acting both on behalf of that court and
the Maltese) he claimed in vain to sign the terms of capitulation of Valetta. Neither Vaubois nor Pigot would agree
to this, the former refusing absolutely to treat with the
Maltese " rebels." Accordingly only the British flag was
hoisted over Valetta, to the great annoyance of the
Neapolitans.[3]

This action of Pigot was due to the Secretary of State,
Henry Dundas, who, on August 1, instructed our commander in the Mediterranean to take all possible steps to
thwart the pretensions of another Power (Russia) which
had of late shown a hostile front, and might, as mistress
of Malta, exclude us from that post.[4] Pigot acted wisely,
according to his lights. To hoist the flag of the Knights

---

[1] " The Paget Papers," i. 256.
[2] Hardman, 331.
[3] Miège, iii. 559.
[4] Hardman, 309, 315-318.

would be to acknowledge the joint ownership of their Grand Master, the Czar. To hoist that of Naples would introduce uncertainty, that court being always liable to pressure from France. As for the flag of the Maltese, no State acknowledged it. Thus Dundas' instructions led to a flag incident of far-reaching import.

We may pause to notice the singular fact that the Christian Powers, which had supported the rule of the Knights of St. John during nearly three centuries, should now suddenly be involved in bitter disputes as to the ownership of the island. Indeed, nowhere did the French revolutionary spirit, incarnate in Bonaparte, hurl the torch of discord into Christendom with more deadly effects. It was the news of his capture of Malta which clinched Russia's resolve to attack the French and thus allied her with Austria, England, and Turkey, the most spectacular result being the advent of a Russo-Turkish fleet in the Aegean. But now, the news that the British flag flew over Valetta threw Paul into a paroxysm of rage, which cost thousands of British seamen in his ports their liberty and their property. Swiftly he turned against us, and formed the Armed Neutrality League. Naples was equally annoyed about Malta, though Grenville assured that court that our occupation was only temporary and did not prejudice the question of ownership. But the Neapolitans took offence, which perhaps explains their agreeing with France in March 1801 to exclude British shipping from all their ports and to admit French troops to the heel of Italy.[1] Alone among the Powers, Turkey desired to see that flag float for ever at Valetta ; for Lord Elgin, our ambassador at Constantinople, soon reported that " The Porte considers her interests and tranquillity secure while England possesses Malta, but not so after our abandoning it." [2] The Knights of St. John raised no pæan of gratitude amidst the general chorus of execration, for the Pitt Ministry, while desirous of handing the island back to them, kept only the British flag flying there.

[1] " Paget Papers," i. 275, 338.   [2] F.O., Turkey, 35.

After the storm of the Armed Neutrality had raged over the Baltic and swept away its Aeolus, the Czar Paul, the British Government made peace with France, agreeing to restore Malta to the Knights. The Czar Alexander I. being on the whole friendly, that plan now presented fewer difficulties. I have found proofs that the Government, at the outset of the negotiations, urged that " the condition of the natives and inhabitants of Malta should be meliorated (*sic*) and that for this purpose admission to the Order and such privileges and immunities should be granted and secured to them as may not be inconsistent with, or derogatory from, the supreme authority of the Knights." Russian troops were to form part of the garrison, customs duties on an equal basis providing means for the defence of Valetta.[1]

It is clear, then, that the Government desired to redress the worst of the grievances of the Maltese under the rule of the Order and to effect a compromise satisfactory both to them, the Knights, the Czar, and even to France. In defending the conditions of peace from the attacks of the Grenvilles and Windham, Pitt stated his regret that we could not retain Malta, but such a step would be too offensive to France.[2] Thus the Maltese compromise of 1801-02 was due to the belief of the Addington Ministry, as also of its supporter, Pitt, that it provided the best means of harmonising the conflicting interests which had of late clashed at Valetta. Primarily the question was international, not Maltese or Neapolitan. The action of Bonaparte in 1798 had opened up a new and dangerous phase of the Eastern question, which centred in Egypt and therefore in Malta. If Russia and England were equally committed to the maintenance of Malta as a bulwark, not of Christendom, but of Europe, then peace might be assured.

We have already seen that the sovereign claims of Naples had practically lapsed during the 270 years of ownership of Malta by the Knights of St. John ; and if the Order could be reconstituted, it was certainly the lawful

[1] F.O., France, 59.        [2] " Parl. History," xxxvi. 60.

owner.  The British Government came to this conclusion
slowly, and its procedure was faulty, the Maltese and
Neapolitan troops being justly irritated at the omission to
recognise their services during the siege and their right to
a share of the prize money.  Ball's abrogation of the
*Consiglio popolare* also gave some offence, though, at a
later date, his capable administration as Governor restored
his popularity.[1]

The outstanding fact, then, is that, after effecting the
surrender of the French garrison, *the British Government did
not annex the island*.  It sought to restore the old order of
things there, by reforming it from within and propping
it from without.  The plan, however, pleased no one,
least of all the Maltese.  They sent to London a deputation
headed by the Marchese Testaferrata, to protest against the
restoration of the Order which, after long misgoverning
them, had treacherously surrendered to the French.  On
March 1, 1802 the deputies proffered a claim for " the
august descendants of Charles V." and the rights of the
islanders.  While disclaiming all desire " to dictate terms
of arrangement," they demanded a just one, and above
all regretted " to be detached from the British Empire "
and placed in a state of neutrality.  In reply Lord Hobart,
Secretary at War and for the Colonies, assured them that
England would do her utmost, and a Maltese Langue was
soon added to the Order.  This drew a grateful acknow-
ledgment, including the admission " that without the
assistance of Great Britain our ruin must have been
inevitable." [2]

The sequel must be noted very briefly.  As is well
known, the Maltese compromise, embodied in Article X. of
the Treaty of Amiens, not only displeased the sensitive
young Czar, but also proved to be unworkable owing to the

[1] Hardman, ch. 23.

[2] Hardman, 420-424.  Why did Azopardi in 1843 say that the Maltese
in 1802 made a voluntary gift of the island to England ?  If in order to
prove that her possession of Malta rested solely on a popular basis, the
argument is weak ; for in 1802 she did not accept Malta, but devolved
it on the Knights, whose rule she sought to improve and popularise.

recent sequestration of the Knights' property by France and Spain in North Italian lands. Naples having sunk under French control since the spring of 1801, a Neapolitan garrison would be no security; and, as Bonaparte was reopening his Mediterranean policy in a very threatening manner, the Addington Government finally demanded the retention of a British garrison in Malta during ten years. Hence ensued a war which desolated Europe during a decade.

In its declaration of war on France in May 1803, the Addington Cabinet declared that " the Order of St. John cannot now be considered as the body to which the island of Malta was to be restored." The statement represented the facts of the case. The confiscation of the property of the Order by France and Spain had signed its death warrant; and its scattered and impoverished members were now unequal to the task of keeping up and defending the very extensive ramparts of Valetta. The British Government had attempted to galvanise that moribund body into life, but had failed. As for the sovereignty of Naples, Napoleon's action in sending French troops into that kingdom was soon to show the impracticability of that solution. His actions supplied the best argument for a British annexation of Malta.

Nelson's last and greatest exploit clinched the matter. In October 1805 the combined fleet of Villeneuve and Gravina received the Emperor's orders to put out from Cadiz, not in order to invade England (as is commonly believed) but to destroy an Anglo-Russian expedition which was endeavouring to assure the safety of South Italy and Sicily. He had earmarked those lands as Napoleonic, in the confident hope that from his Sicilian base he would easily acquire Malta. With this aim in view, he forced out the Franco-Spanish fleet from Cadiz, and the result was Trafalgar. Thereafter the Anglo-Russian force was for a time safe at Naples, and, when forced to evacuate the mainland by the advance of French troops, the British contingent withdrew to Sicily. The persistent efforts of Napoleon to expel it thence reveal the depth of his conviction that the British garrisons in Sicily and Malta constituted *une barrière infranchissable* to his oriental designs.[1]

During nine years the Neapolitan Bourbons, exiles from South Italy, were defended in Sicily by British sailors and soldiers, without whom that contemptible dynasty would have disappeared. At vast expense its duration was assured, and in 1814 it was imposed once more on Naples. If it had some shadowy claims on Malta in 1800, what did they amount to in 1814 ? Certainly the Maltese then had no doubts on the matter, as appears in the inscription in the Great Square at Valetta.

> *Magnae et invictae Britanniae*
> *Melitensium Amor et Europae Vox*
> *Has Insulas confirmat*, A.D. 1814.

---

[1] Napoléon, " Correspondance," No. 10448.

# X

## ADMIRAL DUCKWORTH'S FAILURE AT
## CONSTANTINOPLE IN 1807

IN this article I do not propose to refer to the analogies
which inevitably occur to the mind with the far greater
effort of 1915. But there is one which presents itself at the
outset, viz., a certain similarity of the diplomatic situations
in the winters 1806–07 and 1914–15. At both those periods
we were allied to Russia during a great war, and sought to
further her interests by naval expeditions up the Dardanelles.
Both those attempts were preceded by earnest and reiter-
ated representations to the Porte with a view to dissuading
it from hostilities against Russia. Indeed, much of the
interest attaching to Duckworth's expedition lies in the
controlling authority exerted by a diplomat on board his
squadron, whom Captain Blackwood described " as not only
Minister, but admiral." These words have been quoted as
if they imply praise of the diplomat. The following inquiry
will perhaps throw a different light on his actions and will
raise the question whether the arrangements adopted
for the Dardanelles expedition of February 1807 were
judicious.

That expedition arose out of the following circumstances.
In the autumn of 1806 the rapid extension of Napoleon's
power threatened our allies, Prussia and Russia, with a
complete overthrow. After his victory at Jena he occupied
Berlin, and pursuing the enemy eastwards towards the
Lower Vistula, began to take steps to arouse the Poles
against their Russian and Prussian masters. A natural

157

concomitant was the stirring up of the Turks against the Muscovites—an old device of the Paris Government ; and the French occupation of Dalmatia in accordance with the Austro-French treaty of Pressburg (December 26, 1805) enabled them to bring pressure on the Porte from that quarter.   Napoleon's invasion of Egypt in 1798, and his plans for fomenting Greek risings in the Morea in 1802–03, ought to have rendered him suspect to the Turks, a fact constantly pointed out by the British Government, which could claim to be their best friend.   Nevertheless, hatred of Russia was at this time paramount at the Sublime Porte, because (by virtue of a convention of September 1802) she had imposed on Moldavia and Wallachia *hospodars* friendly to her claims, and was believed to have caused the Serbian revolt of 1806.   In order to utilise to the full the resentment of the Turks, Napoleon, in July 1806, despatched as ambassador General Sébastiani, a clever and active intriguer, whose work in the Orient in 1802 had done much towards precipitating the ensuing rupture with England.   His instructions were to encourage the Turks to be masters everywhere in their Empire (especially in the provinces named above), to close the Bosphorus and all ports to the Russians, and to frame a triple alliance of France, Turkey, and Persia against Russia.   Encouraged by the arrival of Sébastiani, the Porte deposed the Russophile *hospodars* and adopted an attitude of defiance, whereupon the Czar Alexander sent troops to occupy the Danubian provinces, deposed the *hospodars* nominated by the Porte, and demanded the free navigation of the Bosphorus and Dardanelles.   Backed up by Sébastiani, the Turks refused.

The British ambassador at Constantinople, the Rt. Hon. Charles Arbuthnot, had an uphill task to oppose the French, and, even before the news of Jena reached that capital, he wrote to Collingwood, then off Cadiz, requesting the presence of a British squadron in the Dardanelles so as to counteract the influence of Sébastiani and prevent, if possible, its complete triumph.   Collingwood, though at that time hard pressed by the prolonged blockade of a superior force of

Spaniards, yet on November 2 detached Rear-Admiral Sir Thomas Louis with three sail-of-the-line, a frigate, and a sloop, to the Dardanelles.[1] With the " Canopus "[2] (80), and the 74's " Standard " and " Thunderer," and smaller craft, Louis proceeded to Tenedos, and on November 27 entered the straits. By treaty we had the right to navigate the Dardanelles, and he experienced no opposition from the forts at the Narrows. Leaving the "Standard" and "Thunderer" in Azire Bay, he proceeded in the "Canopus," having in company the " Endymion " frigate, which usually acted as guard to the British embassy. The appearance of the two vessels off Constantinople, on November 28, caused for a time considerable alarm at the Porte, especially as Louis did not explain the cause of his mission, and for a time the Sultan behaved most amicably to Arbuthnot, begging his good offices to settle affairs peaceably with Russia. The arrival, however, of the news of Napoleon's advance to the Vistula and his renewed incitements to hostilities against Russia, added to that of the Muscovite invasion of Wallachia, turned the scale, and on December 16 Sébastiani induced the Porte secretly to decide for war with that Power. His arguments failed to induce the same decision against Great Britain. On December 24 the Sultan announced to Italinski, Russian ambassador, the rupture of relations,[3] and the next day he sought refuge on the " Canopus," thereby escaping the sojourn in the Seven Towers, which generally was the lot of ambassadors to Constantinople at the outbreak of war. Louis sailed away on the 28th, leaving the " Endymion " to guard the British embassy and merchants, and soon rejoined the other ships

---

[1] James (iv. p. 213) states that Collingwood acted on orders from home dated October 22. But his letter of November 4 to Lord Howick declares that he did so in consequence of an urgent letter from Arbuthnot (" Collingwood Memoir," p. 251). His letter of November 2 to Louis is far vaguer than his instructions of November 22, which doubtless were in conformity with those from home. See " Papers relative to the Expedition to the Dardanelles," presented to Parliament, March 1808.

[2] The " Canopus " was formerly the " Franklin," taken at the Nile.

[3] E. Driault, " La Politique orientale de Napoléon " (1904), chaps. 2, 3.

in Azire Bay. His attempt at peaceful pressure had failed. His instructions bade him go no further, and in any case he was too weak to exert force effectually. His resolve to leave two sail in the Dardanelles, doubtless as a safeguard against treachery, may be commended. Meanwhile, the British Government, warned by Arbuthnot of the waning of its influence at the Sublime Porte, had decided on stronger measures. On November 21 Lord Howick (formerly First Lord, but now Secretary for Foreign Affairs) instructed the Admiralty, of which Mr. Thomas Grenville was now First Lord, to strengthen Collingwood's fleet, so as to enable him to detach a powerful squadron to Constantinople for the purpose of making vigorous representations to the Porte, and if these should fail " to act offensively against Constantinople." The admiral in command must insist on the release of the British ambassador and all persons belonging to the British factory, in case they had been forcibly detained ; and he was further " to be guided by his communications with him in respect to his future proceedings." Thus, in regard to all questions of policy, that officer was to be the executant of the British ambassador—a fact well to be noted.[1] The Admiralty on November 22 ordered the despatch of six sail to Collingwood, directing him to send Vice-Admiral Sir John Duckworth with an adequate squadron to reinforce Louis, and Grenville warned Collingwood " to leave much to the discretion of that able officer." [2] It is possible that, if Duckworth could have arrived off Constantinople before December 16, the pressure of the sea power would have turned the scale. Also, had the strong Russian squadron in the Adriatic, under Admiral Seniavin, been in friendly communication with Collingwood, it might have shared in Louis' demonstration, which was intended mainly to support Russia. But Seniavin always held aloof, and Collingwood's letter to him, of about

---

[1] " Papers on the Dardanelles," No. 1 (enclosure). As will duly appear, these instructions did not reach Arbuthnot and Duckworth until February 6, 1807, off the Dardanelles.

[2] " Collingwood Memoir," p. 266.

January 12, 1807, did not bring him on to the scene of action in time. Consequently, the expedition, undertaken out of regard for Russia's interests, had no support from that Power. The fact deserves to be remembered, as it disposes of the Czar's peevish complaints at Tilsit, in July, 1807, that England had done nothing to help him.[1]

The reinforcement from England did not reach Collingwood, off Cadiz, until January 12, and not till three days later could he despatch Duckworth eastward with the "Royal George" (100), "Windsor Castle" (98), "Repulse" (74), "Ajax" (74), with the smaller craft "Nautilus" and "Delight," also to take Louis's squadron under his command. Meanwhile, the Russian forces had occupied Bukharest, and for Turkey war had become a question of honour. Collingwood's secret instructions of January 13 to Duckworth, embodying those of the Government, held out the prospect of a peaceful settlement at Constantinople, but bade him act " as circumstances and the state of affairs on his arrival may make necessary." If, however, Arbuthnot's representations to the Porte should fail, " you are to act offensively against Constantinople." If in such a case the Turks seek to negotiate, this is to be regarded as probably a device to gain time, and (says Collingwood) " I would recommend that no negotiation be continued more than half an hour." In case of an absolute refusal he will bombard Constantinople or attack the Turkish fleet and capture or destroy it. In the event of hostilities he will at once inform General Fox, commanding the British forces in Sicily, with a view to the capture of Alexandria. Collingwood further repeated Howick's instruction as to Duckworth being guided by Arbuthnot, but he expressed a hope that " in your ability a resource will be found for every contingency." Apparently on his own responsibility, Collingwood recommended the occupation of the Island of Milo as the best naval base if hostilities occurred.

Obviously, this was a mission of very great difficulty, for

[1] J. H. Rose, " Life of Napoleon I.," p. 127.

Collingwood bids him to defer to Arbuthnot's judgement and yet solve difficulties by his own resourcefulness. How entirely those two men had to rely on themselves appears from these facts, that Arbuthnot, writing at Pera on January 15, 1807, to Lord Howick, states that he knows nothing as to the aims of British policy ; for

" It is now two and a half years since I received any instructions from His Majesty's Government ; for the few lines which were written to me when I was ordered to make the treaty can scarcely be noticed, and so great and various have been the changes during that eventful period that to be considered as having acted always right is what I earnestly wish but can scarcely hope for." [1]

Thus the situation was peculiar. A sailor who was taken from Eton and sent to sea at the age of 11 was to solve a knotty political problem, partly by his own resourcefulness, partly by the directions of an ambassador who had received no instructions from his Government during two and a half years. The frequent changes of Ministers at Westminster added to his perplexity. In point of fact, Howick wrote to him on January 13, commending his actions, expressing a hope for a peaceful settlement, for which purpose Arbuthnot was to offer his mediation, but giving him a free hand in circumstances which may change from day to day. Howick also stated his satisfaction at Louis's expedition up the Dardanelles. But, of course, this despatch arrived too late to decide Arbuthnot's course of action.

In a second despatch of January 15 that ambassador reported that the Turks were likely to offer a stout resistance to the Russians, either on the Danube or on the Balkans, but that if the Czar could send troops to land near the northern end of the Bosphorus, Constantinople would soon fall. Russia's reliance on a revolt of the Janissaries was, however, misplaced. I must now quote the greater part of that despatch, and of a third of the same date :

---

[1] F.O., Turkey, Arbuthnot to Howick, January 13, 1807. Arbuthnot's letters, quoted in the sequel, are from this volume.

" The difficulty of sailing through the Dardanelles, at least in their present defenceless state, would not, I believe, be great. It may be doubted whether the spirit of enterprise which such expeditions would require is to be expected from the Russians. It is only in the equipment of the Turkish fleet that any military preparations are yet to be seen. Seven ships-of-the-line and seven frigates are called in readiness for sea, but seamen of no kind can be obtained to man them. Orders have been given to collect as many as possible in the islands of the Archipelago ; but this will be a work of time and difficulty. Admiral Louis, who saw the Turkish ships of war when acting with us on the coast of Egypt, is astonished at the change for the worse which has since taken place. But the Capitan Pacha of that day was a man of enterprise and ability, and his two immediate successors have been totally inefficient. . . . The Persian who was to proceed from hence on an embassy to Bonaparte has begun his journey in company with Joubert."

Pera, January 15, 1807.—[He has advised Admiral Louis to anchor at Tenedos. The Porte would probably side with the French but for the fear of our ships. Sébastiani (who has been three times at the Porte since the declaration of war) has offered all kinds of help from France.] " It is impossible for me to calculate upon the effects which the King's mediation, provided His Majesty chose to offer it, would produce. In conformity, however, to my former sentiments, I cannot but think that almost any terms with Russia could be still submitted to if the certain alternative were either peace with that Power or war with England. Our Navy is even more dreaded than the armies of France. The Turks expect that the day will come when their European provinces will be lost, and they therefore look to Asia as their best resource, and they feel that that more valuable part of their Empire is more open to the naval attacks of Great Britain than to the land attacks of France."

After this highly interesting statement, which throws a flood of light on Anglo-Turkish relations, Arbuthnot penned no despatch until January 27. Then he wrote his last from Pera, informing Howick that he had received his despatches of November 14, 1806, and rejoiced that his former conduct was approved. At once he requested a conference with the

Porte, and pointed out to the Turkish Ministers the firm
attitude of the British Government, even declaring that he
would prepare for the departure of the British merchants.
The Turkish Ministers were very dejected at this stiff
remonstrance.  They now (said Arbuthnot) believed us to
be serious.

In reality they were preparing a *coup*, for Arbuthnot's
next despatch was written in H.M.S. " Canopus," off
Tenedos, on February 3.  In it he stated that his application for a firman for a safe conduct for his despatches was
refused by the Porte on January 27.  He was about to
advise Captain Capel of the " Endymion " to take them
without a firman ; but, meanwhile, he heard secret news
that the Porte was elated by the news of a great Russian
defeat on December 22, and had resolved to detain the
" Endymion," as also himself and the British merchants as
hostages, also that Sébastiani had been asked to advise as
to the sites of batteries near Constantinople, and the best
stations for the Turkish ships.  Arbuthnot with great
difficulty removed his family and the British merchants
to the " Endymion " before the Turks could carry out their
design of seizing her, and she escaped to H.M.'s squadron
off the Dardanelles.  Fortunately, Admiral Louis's squadron was still in sight of the Turkish ships.  He (Arbuthnot)
left behind a note, dated H.M.S. " Endymion," off the
Seraglio, January 29, protesting against the constraints put
upon him, and stating that Turkey clearly did not desire to
preserve friendly relations with Great Britain.  He would
therefore repair to the British fleet,

" where he can find the security which is refused to him
here ; and it will rejoice him if the Sublime Porte should
send to him such an answer to the demands he made in the
conference of the 25th [27th ?] inst. as will permit his again
returning to his post.  The undersigned will wait a reasonable time before more effectual measures are resorted to for
obtaining redress for the injuries committed against His
Majesty and against his ally, the Emperor of Russia ; but
the Sublime Porte must be aware that her answer can easily
be given without delay.  To the demands made by the

undersigned a plain ' Yes ' or ' No ' is all that is wanted.—
Ch. Arbuthnot.''

This despatch shows that the ambassador had good
reason for his flight, which was not of the unreasonable
character stated by James (iv. p. 215). Rear-Admiral
Louis's long despatch of February 5, 1807 (printed in the
Parliamentary Papers) also shows that the ambassador's
conduct was justifiable, and his subsequent behaviour, as
set forth in the following hitherto unpublished despatches,
evinced no sign of fear.   An ambassador is bound to retire
from a capital when the authorities there prevent his com-
municating with his Government.

The following hitherto unpublished despatches, given
almost in full, will supplement at several points the information given in the " Papers relative to the Dardanelles,
presented to Parliament (March 23, 1808)." In the docu-
ment to Lord Howick, marked private, and dated " Endymion," February 10, at night—

Arbuthnot describes at great length all that happened
since his last letter was sent off.   On the 6th inst. they were
joined by H.M.S. " Active " (Capt. Mowbray), with the
F.O. Instructions of November 20 and a letter from Admiral
Duckworth, who had arrived at Malta with his squadron
and was about to sail to the Dardanelles.   He (Arbuthnot)
had received no answer from the Porte ;  but through the
dragoman Pisani, who, by his permission, had left the
squadron, and was on shore at the Dardanelles, he proposed
a friendly meeting on shore with the Capitan Pacha.   No
answer was received, but he again wrote, pointing out that
" the British Fleet must at all events go up to Constantinople, but that it should depend on him whether we went
thither as friends or foes.''   He then gave reasons for
departing from H.M.'s Instructions, so as to make full use
of the fine fleet which had been sent to give weight to his
representations.   Great Britain might now go further than
was warranted by the Instructions, as the Porte had
adopted a hostile attitude, and we must now exact " a solid
and adequate security," such as will prevent Turkey " from
becoming again the tool of France."   A letter had just
arrived from the Capitan Pacha proposing an interview at

the Castle of the Dardanelles, on the Asiatic side.   But Sir Theo. Louis and Admiral Duckworth (the latter arrived just before his reply was despatched) thought it unsafe for him to enter a Turkish fortress.   "It was resolved between us that he (Admiral Duckworth) should weigh anchor with the whole squadron about three hours after it might be expected that I had gone on shore ;  and the instant that he had been made acquainted with the result of the conference he would then be ready either to force his passage through the Dardanelles or to proceed to Constantinople in a friendly manner, according to the reception which I should give him reason to expect. . . .  I am thoroughly convinced that his (Admiral Duckworth's) measures will be equally guided by vigour and sound judgement.   Indeed, I think myself highly fortunate in having him to act with."

In view of the firm tone of the Instructions from the Foreign Office which he received on February 6, and of the indignities to which the Porte had subjected him, it is rather surprising that Arbuthnot should have made any overture whatever to the Capitan Pacha, and not have instructed Duckworth to proceed up the Dardanelles at once. It was clear that the Turkish forts were being strengthened. The " Pompée," flying the flag of Rear-Admiral Sir Sidney Smith, having joined him, Duckworth now had under his command eight sail-of-the-line, two frigates, and two bomb-vessels, of faulty construction, having their magazines above the water line.   The force was barely adequate to the task, and Louis, on February 5, wrote to Collingwood stating that at least ten sail-of-the-line, a proportionate number of frigates and smaller vessels, " and some troops for the purpose of an occasional *coup de main* where necessary, or to garrison the castles at the Dardanelles (Abydos), while the other (Sestos), which is neither tenable or necessary to possess, might be destroyed, as well as any other points that might occur in the conducting the general service." Louis's experience in the Dardanelles added weight to his decision that troops were a necessity for holding the Narrows, if the expedition was to succeed.   He probably communicated these views to Duckworth, and, as that

admiral had no troops on board except the ordinary complement of marines, this fact accounts for the cautious, not
to say apprehensive, tone of his letters of February 14 to
Collingwood.  He viewed his original enterprise as completely altered in character, and now " the most arduous
and doubtful that had ever been undertaken. . . . We are
to enter a sea environed with enemies, without a possible
resource but in ourselves, and when we are to return there
cannot remain a doubt but that the passage will be rendered
as formidable as the efforts of the Turkish Empire, directed
and assisted by their allies, the French, can make it."  He
concluded, however, that he would make the attempt with
all the means in his power.

James, with his persistent bias against Duckworth, calls
this letter " stuffing a cushion for his fall."  On the contrary, it expressed the prudent prescience of a man who saw
that to attempt to force the Dardanelles and coerce the
Turks at their capital was a most hazardous enterprise, unless
he had an adequate number of vessels and men to enable
him to guard the Narrows while he was in the Sea of
Marmora.  The winds being unfavourable for the attempt,
Duckworth remained at anchor off Tenedos from February
10 to 19, and on the night of the 14th the " Ajax " caught
fire and finally blew up with the loss of 252 lives.  Captain
Blackwood, her commander, and his chief officers thenceforth assisted Duckworth on the " Royal George."  This
unfortunate accident reduced their fighting force to seven
units.  Worst of all, the winds remained foul, and in the
delay of nine days off Tenedos the Turks considerably
strengthened their works, Arbuthnot having during the
conference informed the Capitan Pacha that in any case
the British fleet would proceed to Constantinople.  The
next despatches (partly in précis) from Arbuthnot to Lord
Howick illustrate the situation :

" Royal George," off Tenedos, *February* 14, 1807.

On February 11 a gale prevented his landing for the
proposed interview, and, as the forts fired on the

"Endymion," the effort to land was not made. He, however, made one more effort to come to a friendly understanding, by an interview with the Capitan Pacha at the Outer Castle, on the Asiatic side. That official (though friendly in tone) could not agree to his terms, but wished him [A.] to go with him on the "Endymion" to Constantinople. To that A. would not agree. Other proposals failed. Admiral Duckworth therefore decided to force the Dardanelles before we again attempted to negotiate. "But it is to be recollected that ever since the commencement of the war with Russia this Government has been increasing, and to a great extent, its means of defence; and, should the Turkish Navy have been removed into the Bosphorus, there would, I imagine, be an absolute impossibility of withdrawing it from under the new and strong batteries which, under the inspection of General Sébastiani, have been now erected. I mention this because it is not unlikely that there may be a failure in some of the objects which we have in view. This apprehension, however, would have no effect on the decision of the Admiral, or, if I may say so, on that of myself."

"Royal George," off the Dardanelles, *February* 15, 1807.

H.M.S. "Ajax" has been burnt, about 300 of the crew being saved, but the others have perished. The fleet anxiously awaits a favourable wind to proceed up the Dardanelles. Even if the French victories over the Russians were as great as the French represented, it would still be their duty to act with as much energy as when he (A.) first wrote to England for a naval force. For, if Russia be hard pressed, the more need has she to have her war with Turkey ended. "It is evident from your lordship's instructions that to support the falling interests of H.M.'s ally is one chief object of Sir John Duckworth's fleet; and, whether we succeed or fail, the attempt must surely be made to turn the tide of fortune in the Emperor of Russia's favour." But, as peace is the supreme object, he (Arbuthnot) will not insist " too strenuously on all that I have been directed to demand. . . . I am not afraid of responsibility, but, having in a great measure to decide the serious question of war or peace, I should be the most wretched of all men if from an error of judgment I had hereafter to reproach myself for all the misery which may ensue."

*Ibid., February* 17, 1807.

"  . . . So much time has now elapsed since this
Government was first put upon its guard, that the work to
be effected by Sir John Duckworth is obviously become a
most hazardous and arduous undertaking. . . . The Porte
has been elated by the rapidly increased strength of her
preparations ; and, influenced by the astonishing victories
of Bonaparte, she has evidently placed herself entirely
under General Sébastiani's sole direction.   It is to be seen
whether the arrival of our fleet before Constantinople will
not give rise to other sentiments."

At last, on February 19, the wind shifted to south-south-
west, and the squadron entered the straits.   The outer
Turkish castles of Europe and Asia opened fire on him, but
in deference to Arbuthnot's representations he forbade
from replying.   This forbearance ceased when he was
fired on from the two castles of Sestos and Abydos at the
Narrows, each of which carried three tiers of heavy guns.
They did considerable damage to the leading ship
"Canopus," and for a time the situation was somewhat
critical.   The wind fell so light (so wrote Crawford, the
signal-midshipman on the "Royal George"[1]) that the
ships did little more than stem the current, and the huge
stone balls of the heaviest Turkish guns made nasty gashes
in the leading ships.   These, however, replied so vigorously
as finally to overpower the Turkish gunners, who did little
damage to the rear ships.   The squadron took more than
half an hour to pass those two castles.   In the small bay
north-east of Abydos Castle, on the Asiatic shore, a Turkish
squadron was moored,[2] just under Point Pesquies, on which
a new battery was being erected.   The British ships
cannonaded the Turkish sail in passing, and Sidney Smith
in the "Pompée," with the rear ships "Thunderer" and
"Standard," and the "Active" frigate, hove-to to
complete the work of destruction.   All the Turkish craft

[1] Capt. A. Crawford, R.N., "Reminiscences of a Naval Officer"
(1851), vol. i. ch. 9.
[2] A plan in F.O., Turkey (1807), shows the squadron on the European
side ; but all the accounts imply the Asiatic side.

but one cut their cables and drifted ashore, the crews leaping overboard.[1] In less than four hours he destroyed one ship of 64 guns, four frigates, three corvettes, one brig, and two gunboats, capturing one corvette and one gunboat, which were subsequently found to be useful. The marines and boats' crews of the rear division, under the command of Captain Nichols of the " Standard's " marines, then landed and spiked the thirty guns of the new battery on Point Pesquies. At 5.15 the whole force proceeded on its way, and at 10 P.M. of the next day, February 20, anchored near the Prince's Isles, eight miles below Constantinople. Duckworth then despatched Captain Capel in the " Endymion " to anchor near that city, so as to convey the ambassador's despatches to the Porte next morning under a flag of truce ; but, the wind failing, Capel could not stem the current and anchored four miles away at 11.30 P.M.[2]

Considering that the Turks had opened fire from all the forts in the Dardanelles, the effort of Arbuthnot to negotiate is inexplicable. Collingwood's instructions of January 13 bade Duckworth act offensively against Constantinople, in case the ambassador's representations to the Porte should fail, and added a special caution against a lengthy negotiation, which was not to exceed half an hour. This last was Collingwood's own recommendation, but it had almost the force of a command. Arbuthnot also, on February 3, had demanded a plain " Yes " or " No," and, though he received no answer in words, yet it came in shots from the Turkish forts of the Dardanelles. As the Capitan Pacha was reported to have come from Constantinople and almost certainly acted according to orders from the capital, the Turks had deliberately committed an act of war and should have been treated accordingly. But Arbuthnot was now ill in his hammock on the " Royal

---

[1] The " Moniteur " of April 15 asserted that the Turkish crews were away celebrating the feast of Bairam ; and that the British, irritated by some shots they had received, attacked the almost defenceless Turkish ships, " commettant un de ces crimes dont cette nation seule est capable " !

[2] " Papers on the Dardanelles," Duckworth to Collingwood, February 21, 1807.

George," and seems to have been upset by the load of
responsibility.  He therefore counselled a further negotiation, which indeed he had promised the Capitan Pacha to
undertake.  As the lack of wind rendered an approach to
Constantinople impossible, Duckworth probably did not
go far wrong in complying.  But he certainly should have
taken every precaution against treachery and should have
fortified temporarily the most commanding positions on
the Prince's Islands.  He seems to have trusted to the
suggested negotiation, and both of them considered it
fortunate that they had not gone close in, " as a nearer
approach might have given cause for suspicion and alarm." [1]
Such is the extraordinary statement by Duckworth himself.
In the sentences following he says nothing about the
British overture of February 21 failing, but this is affirmed
both in Arbuthnot's and Crawford's accounts, the former
asserting that during five or six hours on the 22nd the wind
favoured an approach to the capital.  It may be well,
however, to cite or summarise his despatch to Lord Howick
F.O. Turkey (1807)

" Royal George," off the Dardanelles, *March* 6, 1807.

[After stating that illness prevented him dictating more
than a few lines, he continues :—]
" . . . I shall therefore say that a full idea was now
given to me of what British officers and seamen are able to
effect.  Had there not been as much coolness as animation
in combat, it would have been almost impossible during
so heavy a fire to carry a squadron safe through so narrow
and intricate a passage.  The Vice-Admiral certainly
added much to his former reputation by his conduct on
this occasion."  He then recounts the events before
Constantinople.  As the Turks had believed the passage
impossible, they had not greatly fortified the approaches
to Constantinople ; and, had the wind not failed on
February 21, we should have caused a panic in the city.
On the 22nd Isaac Bey arrived on board and begged us not
to weigh anchor and approach the city, as otherwise a
rising and massacre would ensue.  When the negotiations

[1] *Ibid.* Duckworth to Collingwood, March 6, 1807.

failed, the Admiral said he would proceed. But the wind then failed. " It was only on the 22nd for the short space of five or six hours [1] that the squadron could stem the current and move towards Constantinople ; and, with the knowledge I had of H.M.'s pacific intentions, and, indeed, according to the instructions I had received, it seemed to me impossible that some short interval should not be allowed to the Turkish Government to make its choice."

" . . . It was highly fortunate that we should be favoured by the wind, which enabled us to repass the Dardanelles. It is astonishing how well the Turks had employed the interval ; for, although in coming back we had a much stronger wind and the current in our favour, the damage to the squadron was unfortunately far greater."

One can pardon much to a sick man, but this account is exceedingly meagre. From Duckworth's despatch of the same date it appears that for " a few hours " on Sunday, February 22, he prepared to advance, but the uncertainty of the weather, " and the Minister's desire that I should give a few hours for an answer to his letter through Isaac Bey, prevented me from trying. Before 5 P.M. it was nearly calm, and in the evening the wind was entirely from the eastward, and continued light airs or calm till the evening of the 28th, when it blew fresh from the north-east and rendered it impossible to change our position." Crawford also describes the eagerness of the crews on the morning of the 22nd, when, there being " a commanding breeze from the southward, everything looked as it ought, and as if we were going at it in right earnest." But soon after noon, when all was ready, a boat hove in sight with Isaac Bey, " an elderly gentleman with a grave and solemn aspect." Isaac was closeted an hour and a half with Arbuthnot, and at his departure all warlike preparations were suspended. Isaac came again (says Crawford) the next day, and had an interview lasting two hours. After that Isaac came no more.

It seems incredible that the ambassador, who knew the

---

[1] In his last despatch, of June 6, he says it was only three hours that the wind was favourable.

ways of Orientals, or even Duckworth, who knew them
not, should have been taken in by this obvious device.
But apparently both were gulled. Duckworth reflected with
much satisfaction that a British "project" was forwarded
through the medium of Isaac on the 22nd, and that every
step had been taken to evince the pacific disposition of the
British Government. Had he perused once more Collingwood's instructions he could scarcely have been drawn
into this Turkish snare. By the 27th the Turks had
recovered from their panic. But at first the panic, which
Duckworth deemed it so desirable to assuage, had been
excessive. Sébastiani wrote to Paris that the Turks would
give in to all the British conditions, and he added : " Non
seulement on me donnera l'ordre de quitter Constantinople,
mais, si les Anglais le désirent, on me mettra aux Sept
Tours." But the versatile Frenchman soon recovered his
aplomb. He it was, apparently, who primed Isaac for his
mission, and advised the construction of coast batteries, " as
if by a fairy's wand," so that he boasted on February 27
that 520 cannon and 110 mortars were in position.[1] On
the 28th the Turks repulsed a British party landing on
Prota Island to dislodge its defenders, and on March 1
Duckworth's squadron made for the Dardanelles.

His decision to make use of the northerly wind was
undoubtedly wise. The Turks were certain to strengthen
the Dardanelles forts, and Duckworth had been able to
spare only the " Active " and the captured Turkish
corvette to guard the passage ; but what could two small
vessels do against the Turkish reinforcements that poured
in ? Having no landing force there to hold the commanding position on Pesquies Point, he might be over-
whelmed if the battery there had been re-armed.
Fortunately, it was not, and the squadron anchored and
passed the night of March 1-2 without disturbance just
above that promontory. On the morrow, despite the
favouring northerly wind and the current, the squadron
suffered considerably from the fire of the castles of Sestos

[1] Driault, *op. cit.* pp. 95-103.

and Abydos.   A marble ball, weighing 850 lb., struck the "Windsor Castle," glanced up between decks and cut through two-thirds of the main mast, which was with difficulty kept standing.   Our losses were 29 killed, 138 wounded, as against 10 killed and 77 wounded in the far longer passage up the Narrows on February 19.

The strictly naval part of Duckworth's achievement was creditable.   Where he failed was in the difficult sphere of politics.   Doubtless, it was unwise in the home Government to bind his hands by bidding him refer to the ambassador on all political questions.   Howick did not see that political and naval questions interlocked, and that where they did so the admiral should have had the last word.   His successor, Thomas Grenville, added a tactful modification of those instructions, and Collingwood acted shrewdly in recommending Duckworth not to let a negotiation drag on for more than half an hour, and if Collingwood's advice had been followed on the critical day, February 22, all would have gone well.   Instead, Duckworth deferred to the wishes of Arbuthnot, who, in his deplorable state of health, was likely to counsel a tame procedure.   The result was deplorable.   Instead of bringing the Turks sharply to their senses, Duckworth delayed, and finally had to retire amid the derision of the Orientals, and with results fatal to British prestige in the East.   But, after all, he was less blameworthy than the ambassador.   Arbuthnot forgot that naval and diplomatic considerations were, on the 22nd, inextricably mingled.   Yet he took upon him to put aside the naval in favour of the diplomatic factor, with the results that have been seen.   Later on, after returning home, he wrote the following letter to the new Foreign Secretary, George Canning :—

London, *June* 6, 1807.

[After giving at length a résumé of his proceedings (as his former despatches were curtailed owing to illness) he adds] : " . . . I trust it will be felt generally that I was not too eager to act in the first instance, nor over-cautious afterwards ; but I must, however, in fairness, confess that

it was I who advised the expedition, it was I who led H.M.'s
late Ministers to believe that in all human probability it
would be successful ; and it was I who thought it ad-
visable, notwithstanding the change of circumstances which
had arisen, that the effort originally intended should still
be made."

A full account of events at the Dardanelles follows.   At
his second interview with Sir John Duckworth the latter
avowed that, having gained new information (chiefly from
Arbuthnot's despatches, " the whole undertaking appeared
to him (Duckworth) far more arduous, and the success
much less certain, than he had originally imagined. . . ."

" . . . As I had learnt from my dragoman, Mr. Pisani,
that there was no great activity displayed in erecting the
new batteries at the Dardanelles ; and as I had letters in
my pocket from Sir Thos. Louis, written on January 26, in
which he says that, in spite of opposition, he could proceed
to Constantinople with his much smaller squadron, and
that he was confident of being able to perform that service
with facility,[1] I did on these accounts represent most
forcibly to Sir John Duckworth that we had no alternative
left but that of forcing the passage.  The Admiral, after
having thus properly pointed out the danger to be
apprehended, not only acquiesced most readily in my
reasoning, but he went so far as to say that, according
entirely in opinion with me, he had been all along determined to force the passage at all risks and hazards. . . . I
must in justice declare that, should our passing the
Dardanelles be now considered to have been imprudent, it
is I, and not the Admiral, who have been in fault ; for he
had no other information to guide him than what he
received from me."  He then testifies to the eagerness of
the Admiral to reach Constantinople ; but while the wind
was adverse he (Arbuthnot) deemed it wise to protract the
negotiation.  Then he was incapacitated by illness, but
he sent for the officers to ask them whether the fleet could
not make the attempt, as they can testify ; " and if one
amongst them should ever have suspected me, either in
illness or in health, of being inclined to negotiate when it
was more my duty to act, I will then submit to this afflicting
sentence of disgrace which ought in justice to be passed

---

[1] This statement is at variance with that of Louis, in his letter of
February 5 to Collingwood, already summarised in this article.

upon me." Finally, he mentions the awe in which the Turks had held the British Navy, so that in ordinary cases they would have conceded anything to it. "Pisani used figuratively to declare that if our ships attempted to sail up Mt. Olympus the Turks would expect to see it accomplished."

Arbuthnot's candid admission of complete responsibility almost disarms criticism. But even this statement cannot absolve him from censure for his action on February 22.[1] There is no documentary sign of Canning's disapprobation, but Arbuthnot was not employed again in a diplomatic capacity, though he became one of the joint secretaries of the Treasury. Duckworth, though recalled from the Mediterranean, was employed in the Baltic and elsewhere. The contrast is probably significant.

As the Parliamentary Papers on the Dardanelles expedition do not include the correspondence between Duckworth and the Russian Admiral Seniavin, who arrived off Tenedos about a week after the return of the British squadron, I append the following letters. On Duckworth proposing a joint occupation of Tenedos, Seniavin replied by an urgent suggestion that they should together force the Dardanelles and compel Turkey to a peace. In an interview he pressed this matter upon Duckworth, alleging that these were his orders, and that, having 8 sail-of-the-line, he must fulfil them. He then wrote a letter formally requesting British co-operation. To this Duckworth replied as follows :

"Royal George," off the Dardanelles, *March* 10, 1807.

" . . . . Your excellency already knows my sentiments respecting the absolute impossibility of reducing Constantinople, defended as that capital now is, by a naval force alone. Without troops to land we could do no more than lay our ships alongside the numerous and formidable batteries which have been erected. And, although we

---

[1] The evidence now set forth refutes the statement in " Dict. of Nat. Biography " (article Arbuthnot, Ch.) : " It was mainly owing to his firmness that whatever success attended the operation was achieved."

might do some injury to the town, we could not but expect
that our ships would be considerably disabled, and thereby
rendered less capable of effecting our passage when it might
be found necessary to return through the Dardanelles.
Still, however, none of these considerations shall affect me
so far as to make me decline giving the assistance which
your excellency, in conformity to the orders of your Court,
has required of me. . . .

"But before the undertaking is again attempted, there is
one condition on which my duty to my sovereign will oblige
me to insist.   Having passed and repassed the Dardanelles,
and having on the second occasion seen the batteries which
were beginning to be erected, and which, when completed,
as they must be by the present time, would render the work
still more difficult and arduous, I must, as an officer, declare
it to be my decided opinion that, without the co-operation
of a powerful body of land forces, it would be a wanton
sacrifice of the squadrons of both nations to attempt to
force the passage.   I do not pretend to be able to say what
number of troops would be necessary ; but, as your excellency is commander-in-chief of all the military forces of
your sovereign in the Mediterranean, both land and naval,
you can no doubt send for such a proportion of the troops
you have under your command as may be equal to land and
destroy the batteries of the Dardanelles, and, by occupying
the principal posts, to render our return secure.   H.M.'s
squadron under my command has already effected everything that could be expected from a naval force alone, and,
indeed, without speaking presumptuously, I think I may be
allowed to say that, if a British fleet is not able to succeed
in the objects which it has in view, there could not be much
hope that more would be done by the fleet of any other
nation.

"It would indeed have rejoiced me if the four line of
battle ships of your sovereign, which I had been taught to
expect would have been already here previous to my
arrival, had been present to co-operate with me in my late
undertaking.   I feel most confident that I should have
received from them the most effectual assistance ; and, our
appearance off Constantinople being more formidable, we
might, by being able to strike a greater panic, have had
perhaps a better chance of success."

I summarise Seniavin's reply :

A bord du Vaisseau Twerdog, devant les Dardanelles,
Cet 1 le Mars [N.S.], 1807.

He agrees that they cannot occupy Constantinople ; but
it is not impossible—" de forcer une seconde fois les
Dardanelles, d'incendier la capitale et la flotte Ottomane,
d'y augmenter la confusion et le désordre . . . et d'obliger
enfin les Turcs, égarés par des conseils perfides, à revenir à
leur ancien système vis-à-vis de la Russie et de l'Angleterre."
His orders to force a passage are positive. He has here
eight sail-of-line, and a frigate ; he expects two more
sail-of-line, and several smaller vessels. He begs Duckworth to co-operate with six sail-of-line, two frigates, two
bomb-vessels. The Russian forces for landing are 2000
men. He regrets extremely his inability to be present in
time for the first attempt.

In his answer Duckworth states that he adheres to his
first opinion ; also he deems 2000 troops quite inadequate
for the suggested landing in the Dardanelles. The proposed
expedition being impracticable, he declines sharing in it.
Other duties in the Mediterranean may soon call him away.
On February 28/March 12, 1807 Seniavin acknowledges
same with great regret, and says that, if that plan be
impossible, they ought jointly to blockade the Dardanelles
and occupy Tenedos, Lemnos, and Tasso [Thasos ?] so as to
procure provisions, water, and wood ; also to cruise off
the coast of Asia Minor. To this Duckworth replied on
March 13 that this was highly desirable, but, as his squadron
is needed in the West Mediterranean, the Russian force
alone must discharge these duties. Duckworth, in a letter to
Collingwood, stated that Seniavin's proposal was designed
merely to justify himself for desisting from the enterprise.[1]
Arbuthnot, while at Constantinople, had written that
Russia showed little desire to concert her interests with
ours, and Collingwood's feelings towards that Power were
similar.[2] The sequel was to justify their distrust.

The chief interest, however, of the Dardanelles expedition
of February 1807 is the light which it throws on the need

---

[1] " Collingwood Memoir," p. 282.
[2] *Ibid.* p. 277.

of extreme care in the co-ordinating of diplomatic and naval policy. Apart from the sagacious proposal of the First Lord, Thomas Grenville, that much should be left to the discretion of the admiral, the instructions from home were such as to tie Duckworth's hands. At any rate, Arbuthnot, when off Constantinople, directed affairs almost entirely, and Duckworth deferred to him in a manner which, in view of the methods employed by the Turks in beginning hostilities, must be pronounced weak. Fortified by Collingwood's recommendation not to enter into a lengthy negotiation, he should have insisted on an immediate answer while the weather conditions were favourable. The other fact which challenges attention is the conviction formed, both by Louis and Duckworth, that an attempt to coerce the Porte at Constantinople by an expedition up the Dardanelles was madness without the aid of an adequate landing force to guard the Narrows. Very significant was Duckworth's warning to Seniavin : " I must, as an officer, declare it to be my decided opinion that, without the co-operation of a powerful body of land forces, it would be a wanton sacrifice of the squadrons of both nations to attempt to force the passage."

# XI

## CHIVALRY AND THE SEA [1]

I USE the term chivalry here in its wider significance as denoting the qualities of bravery, generosity, and clemency evinced at all times of war or danger ; and the present inquiry is limited to maritime warfare. The first thing which strikes us is the absence of anything approaching to the ideal of chivalry from sea warfare in the ancient world. We may go further and say that coast dwellers, as they looked over the waste of waters, were haunted by perpetual fear—fear not only of what Nature might do in her wilder moods, but also of what man would do under cover of her wing. Not only to the Hebrews, but to all dwellers by the sea that element was the cradle of tempests and the abode of human lawlessness and cruelty. If we turn to the pages of Herodotus, we catch a glimpse of one of the hateful tricks played by seamen on a coast population. In his graphic way he pictures Phoenician traders coming in their round ships to bargain with the Argives. They back their vessels on to a shelving beach, ready to make off speedily, and then bring forth their tempting wares. On the beach they spread their merchandise for five or six days, until a number of women are tempted to come down and buy the Tyrian silks. While they are intent on their bargains, the sailors rush upon them, hurry them into the ship, and sail off with everything—silks, purchasers, and their money. One can scarcely imagine a more profitable transaction, save that it cannot be repeated !

[1] Read to the Royal Literary Society on April 25, 1923.

Thucydides, in his less graphic but more rationalistic way, points out (Book I. ii. 5) that in early times all barter, whether by sea or land, went on under a perpetual fear. Both Greeks and barbarians turned to piracy, under the lead of their most powerful men, and he adds that they did so, not only for their own gain, but also with a view to " maintenance of the needy." One wonders how large a proportion this charitable piracy bore to the genuine article! In any case it is certain that the piratical customs of early times often depopulated the coastal districts, except, of course, where a steep promontory or other natural advantage offered protection to seafaring men and their families. During long ages it was the custom on the coasts to ask strangers whether or no they were pirates. Apparently the question gave no offence, and was fully consonant with primitive etiquette.

Thus, in ancient times there is no trace of chivalry among the maritime peoples. The sea was the abode of lawlessness, perfidy, and violence, except where some powerful ruler like Minos of Crete enforced order by a powerful fleet. Apparently it was he who first enabled a large coast population to grow up in Crete and furthered the spread of peaceful commerce and maritime enterprise. In later times, and in fact down to the age of Sulla, Crete degenerated, and became the abode of pirates, rivalling even Cilicia as the haunt of these pests. They became so powerful as to form a robber State ; and that staid historian, Mommsen, bears tribute to their daring, and even to their chivalrous comradeship. The outcasts of all nations there found places of refuge ; and during several decades this " freemasonry of exile and crime " (as he terms it) bade defiance to Rome. The pirates had their strongholds in the fastnesses of Dalmatia, Cilicia, and Crete, where they reared their families on the spoil of the seas ; and while their hand was against every man, they never failed to come to the aid of a pirate hard pressed.[1]

This rough and cruel knight-errantry is the nearest

[1] Mommsen, iv. 40-41.

approach to chivalry which can be found in the hard and selfish life of the ancient world. Chivalry in its best form is essentially a product of Christianity. Achilles, the pattern of the Greek warrior, behaved no better than a feline to the body of Hector ; and throughout Greek and Roman history we find the lot of the captives horrible. Those taken at sea were generally disposed of at once. " They captured the ship and killed the crew " is a sentence that often recurs in Thucydides ; and it is with something of surprise that we read of the generous treatment of prisoners by the Athenian admiral Phormio, who, after his victory at Naupactus, picked up most of the crews of the twelve Peloponnesian ships that he had rammed, and brought them away with him. The Peloponnesians did not emulate his generosity, for a day or two later, when they cut off nine Athenian ships and drove them on the rocks, they slew every man who did not swim ashore.[1] That was the normal procedure in ancient times.

To exult over the misery of a fallen foe was also quite compatible with good taste. I confess that I find it impossible to read without a strong feeling of disgust Aeschylus' drama, the " Persian Women." In the final scene the presentation of the beaten Persian king, Xerxes, after his flight from the Battle of Salamis, arriving at his royal palace, amidst the wailings of Persian mothers, and their mutual challenges to outdo each other in lamentations, appears to the modern mind one of the most unchivalrous scenes ever devised for the stage ; and all the emphasis which Aeschylus lays on the working of *Até* cannot blind us to this defect. There is no modern poet who, after a great naval victory of his people, would so far demean himself as to represent on the stage his beaten enemies engaging in a wailing contest ; and, if he did, his play would be hissed off the stage. Yet Aeschylus marked the highest level of intellectual and moral achievement at ancient Athens.

What a contrast there is in Shakespeare's treatment of a somewhat similar crisis in our national life. In his budding

[1] Thucydides, ii. 84, 90.

manhood (æt. 24) he heard of the great deliverance of
England from the Spanish Armada ; but his plays contain
no direct reference to it.   Indeed, apart from that glorious
outburst of John of Gaunt—

> this little world,
> This precious stone set in the silver sea—

we should scarcely know from his dramas that

> This blessed plot, this earth, this realm, this England

had of late been in grave danger.   I cannot recall in his
plays a single word of exultation over the Spaniards.   The
difference of outlook from that of Aeschylus is very marked;
and it seems to be due chiefly to a change in the way of
regarding a beaten enemy.   This change, in its turn, was
due to the customs of chivalry.

When we speak of the age of chivalry, our thoughts turn
at once to Froissart and to the reign of Edward III.   Certainly that was the heyday of chivalry on land ; but its
behests counted for nought at sea.   That element was the
abode of robbery and treachery as much as in ancient times.
Scottish pirates often infested the Nore, and fierce hatred
prevailed between English and Normans, as was the rule
between all peoples inhabiting opposite coasts.   The
Normans had sacked and burnt Southampton shortly
before Edward III. began his long war against France.
Thus a bitter enmity rankled in both nations, and imparted
to the first important naval battle, that of Sluys, a peculiar
ferocity :

" This battle (says Froissart) was right fierce and
horrible ; for battles by sea are more dangerous and fiercer
than battles by land ; for at sea there is no retreat or flee-
ing ; there is no remedy but to fight and abide fortune,
and every man to show his prowess."

Under these euphemisms there lurks a horrible truth—
that the conflict ended in indiscriminate slaughter or drown-
ing of prisoners.   Such was the case somewhat later in the
sharp fight with the Spanish fleet off Rochelle.   There both
sides pitched overboard all the survivors on the captured

ships ; and this seems to have been the usual practice at the
end of desperate naval fights.  Knights and men-at-arms
shared the same fate as the common seamen.  A sea-fight
was " your great leveller."  In this connection we should
remember that the very small size of ships then, and long
after, told against the preservation of prisoners.  There
was little room in which to stow them, and still less food
and water to spare for them.  To pitch them overboard
was the obvious expedient ; and it took long ages of
improvement both in ships and morality to introduce the
code of chivalry to sea warfare.

Such, then, was life at sea in olden times.  It was cruel,
treacherous—utterly opposed to the ideals and practice of
chivalry.  In Chaucer's merry company of pilgrims the
shipman of Dartmouth is a forbidding figure, with " mur-
derer " stamped on his brutal features.  He is the product
of the seamanship of that age.  And down to the times of
Shakespeare that type abounded.  At the end of " Othello,"
Lodovico speaks thus to Iago :

> O Spartan dog,
> More fell than anguish, hunger, or the sea !

It is not easy to say when the ideas of chivalry began to
extend to maritime warfare.  Certainly it was far later
than on land.  We usually think of the Emperor Charles
V. as hard-hearted and obstinate, but not needlessly cruel.
Yet in his reign, and almost certainly by his orders, instructions were issued to captains of Spanish ships to throw
overboard the crews of all other ships which ventured into
the Spanish waters.  And Philip II. of Spain in 1557
ordered that, on the capture of such "interlopers," the
officers were to be hanged and the seamen sent to the
galleys for life.  Even in 1587, the year before the Armada,
the Spanish commander-in-chief, Santa Cruz, had orders to
kill every man found on board any English ship.[1]  That
order, be it observed, concerned regular warfare on the
ocean, not the catching of interlopers in the Spanish seas.

[1] M. Oppenheim, Note in " Sir W. Monson's Naval Tracts," vol. i.
p. 202 (Navy Records Society).

Whether the Spanish admirals in 1587 or in 1588 meant to carry out this ferocious order I am not aware, for the reason that we gave them no chance. The captures were all on the other side. It appears that the English sometimes killed or threw overboard their prisoners taken at sea, especially when they would prove an encumbrance. On the other hand, the lives of Spanish captives were often spared ; witness the case of the " Nuestra Señora del Rosario," whose officers and men were taken to Torbay ; whereat the Sheriff of Devon was none too well pleased, and remarked with gruff humour that it was a pity they had not " been made water spaniels." So, too, Hakluyt, in his account of the Spanish Armada, records the generous treatment of the Spanish officer, Admiral Valdez, by Drake. Valdez' ship had been cut off and finally surrendered to Drake, partly because Valdez knew of Drake's chivalry. Thereupon Drake " embraced him, and gave him very honourable entertainment, feeding him at his own table and lodging him in his cabin." [1]

Be it remembered, then, that the Elizabethan age, despite instances to the contrary, does exhibit cases where the victors treat the vanquished crews with clemency ; and that magnanimous virtue (it seems to me) is by far the most important contribution which chivalry has made towards the progress of mankind. So soon as the practice of forbearance towards captives taken at sea began to spread, maritime customs gradually lost much of their old-world ferocity and faithlessness. The uplift towards generosity and good faith took place slowly, of course, and there were many lapses, especially in distant waters, where the ideas of law and justice penetrate slowly, if at all. But from the time of Elizabeth we may date the beginnings of a better age, when the sea became less and less the abode of rapine and treachery, and more and more the arena of chivalrous adventure.

The age of the great maritime discoveries ought to have witnessed the growth of a world-wide sentiment of generous

[1] Hakluyt, ii. p. 384.

enterprise ; for could anything appeal more strongly to
the best feelings in man than the setting out of Columbus
in three small caravels ?   And the voyages of Vasco da
Gama, Magellan, the Cabots, and others were inspired by
the same generous spirit which spurred on the Argonauts,
aye, and all true explorers, from that remote age to the age
of Amundsen, Scott, and Shackleton.   Yet it is undeniable
that the sequel to the efforts of Columbus and his compeers
was far from chivalrous.   How are we to 'explain this
curious fact ?   Largely, I think, because the Papal Bull of
1493, followed by the Treaty of Tordesillas, divided the
newly discovered lands between Spain and Portugal.   This
partition introduced the feeling of exclusive ownership in
its narrowest form, with the result that political jealousies
became keen, and led to the most odious devices for keeping out all competitors.   The lust of gold also came in
to excite private cupidity.   Consequently the discovery
of the New World, which ought speedily to have brought
untold blessings to the Old World, served but to excite the
rivalries and inflame the passions of all the maritime peoples,
thereby postponing for a century the growth of those generous instincts which spring from competition in adventure.
Such feelings doubtless inspired many of the early Spanish
and Portuguese explorers ; but they were half choked by
monopolist greed.

On the whole it seems safe to say that the spirit of maritime chivalry first appears most strikingly in the best of
the English adventurers who were resolved to break down
the Spanish monopoly.   That spirit is incarnate in Drake.
It has been set forth with wealth of imagery by Mr. Noyes.
Thus is it that he pictures the start on the great voyage for
the Pacific (1577) :

> So on a misty grey December morn
> Five ships put out from calm old Plymouth Sound.
> Five little ships, the largest not so large
> As many a coasting yacht or fishing trawl
> To-day ; yet these must brave uncharted seas
> Of unimagined terrors, haunted glooms
> And shadowy horrors of an unknown world

Wild as primaeval chaos.   In the first,
The " Golden Hinde," a ship of eighteen guns,
Drake sailed.

   \*        \*        \*        \*        \*

Their crews, all told, were eight score men and boys.

The poet follows them on their wondrous quest, and
richly embroiders every striking incident.  The treachery
of Doughty, and his condemnation by the crew's acclaim,
in that lonely bay of Patagonia, where still clanked the
chain on the gibbet erected by Magellan fifty years before
for the execution of one of his traitors—the solemn taking
of the communion together by Drake and Doughty as the
day waned to the hour of doom—

                     The great sun dropped
Suddenly, and the land and sea were dark ;
And as it were a sign Drake lifted up
The gleaming sword.   It seemed to sweep the heavens
Down in its arc as he smote once, and no more.

   \*        \*        \*        \*        \*

And a great shout went up,—" So perish all
Traitors to God and England."

All this is grandly told, as befits a grand theme.   Never
before or since, surely, have captain and conspirator (for I
cannot accept a modern version that exculpates Doughty)
taken the communion together like Christian brothers,
and then feasted and conversed together, even while both
knew that the one and only possible ending for the arch-
mutineer was nigh at hand.[1]  Drake was inexorably stern,
as he had to be ;  but, so far as could be, he softened the
bitterness of death for one whom he had loved as a comrade
in chivalry.

Those were great times.   Narrow ideas still cramped the
minds of men ;  but the men were great and soon burst
through the rind of tradition and custom.   Consider the
ending of the Spanish Armada.   A pamphlet of the year 1591
thus sums it up :

---

[1] Noyes (vol. i. p. 172) makes the execution almost immediately after
the trial.   Corbett (" Drake and the Tudor Navy," i. 246) shows that
it was two days after.

" With all their so great and terrible an ostentation, they did not, in all their sailing round about England, so much as sink or take one ship, bark, pinnace, or cockboat of ours, or ever burnt so much as one sheepcote of this land."

The writer then describes the magnanimity of Queen Elizabeth towards the Spanish prisoners who were wrecked on the Irish coasts. Many were slain by the natives, but others were captured by the English forces and brought to England—

" Where (says our writer) Her Majesty, of her princely and invincible disposition, disdaining to put them to death, and scorning to retain or entertain them, (they) were all sent back again to their countries, to witness and recount the worthy achievements of their invincible and dreadful Navy."

Such treatment of Spanish prisoners was, perhaps, as politic as it was chivalrous. But it marks an advance in the customs of the time. Furthermore, the gentlemen adventurers of the west country who now took to the sea were true knights of the sea. The Carews, Cobhams, Grenvilles, Horseys, Killigrews, Strangways, and Tremaynes fought for Queen, country, and religion, more than for gain. One of the earlier Grenvilles thus wrote of the passion for maritime adventure :

> Who seeks the way to win renown
> Or flies with wings to high desire,
> Who seeks to wear the laurel crown,
> Or hath the mind that would aspire—
> Let him his native soil eschew,
> Let him go range and seek a new.[1]

This spirit was incarnate in Sir Richard Grenville, the hero of that titanic fight of the " Revenge." He was son of Sir Roger Grenville, a gentleman of the north of Cornwall, who perished on board the " Mary Rose " when she foundered during the fight with the French at Spithead in 1545. The son, Sir Richard, was of a hard and fierce nature,

---

[1] " Sir R. Grenville's Farewell."

devoted to war, and but little loved in peace. In 1588 he served on land, defending part of Cornwall. Perhaps it was his ill luck in not serving at sea with Howard and Drake that made him thirst for maritime renown. So we find him, three years later, shipping with another Howard (Lord Thomas) to make war on the Spaniards at the Azores or in their Indies. His ship was the " Revenge," of nearly 500 tons, and of from 30 to 40 guns. She was a heavily armed ship and was deemed of a most serviceable type— in fact, she was the prototype of our 74's of the age of Rodney and Nelson.

Undoubtedly the " Revenge " was a first-class fighting ship by comparison with the ill-armed ships of the Spanish " Flota." From Terceira they came upon the " Revenge " and her consorts as they were getting ballast and refreshments at Flores in the Azores. Lord Tennyson has told the tale in glorious verse. All we need remember here was that the " Revenge " was last of the English squadron to get out to sea. The other ships escaped from the net which the Spaniards flung around them. But Grenville scorned to fly before them, or even to pass to leeward of them, which would imply giving way before them. There seems some doubt whether he, and he alone, deliberately stayed behind in order to bring off all his comrades who were on shore. For in the fight that ensued he had less than 200 hands aboard (whether sound or sick), and his normal complement was 250.[1] Therefore it seems more likely that he bore to windward of them from mere *punctilio*, or from sheer love of a fight. His master (*i.e.* navigating officer) urged him to let down the courses, or mainsails, and pass quickly to leeward of them, and so escape ; but he swore to kill the first man who touched those sails, and thus, in the afternoon, challenged the Spaniards to attack. Soon the " Revenge " was surrounded. Between their two squadrons she lay, and fought on far into the night. By 3 A.M. she had (it is said) beaten off fifteen Spanish ships ; and as dawn broke, she lay mastless and silent, but still

---

[1] Corbett, ii. 359, note.

defiant to the Spanish ships that lay half crippled around. Grenville, now dying of his wound, ordered the master to blow her up, " that thereby nothing might remain of glorie or victorie to the Spaniards." But at this command there broke out a controversy among officers and men, which ended in the master going off in a boat to the Spanish admiral to surrender :

" Who (writes Linschoten), finding none over hastie to enter the ' Revenge ' again, doubting least Sir Richard would have blowne them up and himself . . . yielded that all their lives should be saved, the company sent to England, and the better sort to pay such reasonable ransom as their estate would beare, and in the mean season to be free from galley or imprisonment."

Linschoten adds that he gave these wholly exceptional terms out of admiration for Sir Richard Grenville. The Spaniards did all in their power for his recovery ; but he died in their midst, with these words on his lips :

" Here die I, Richard Grenville, with a joyful heart and a quiet mind, for that I have ended my life as a good soldier ought to do who has fought for his country, Queen, religion, and honour. Wherefore my soul joyfully departeth out of this body, and shall always leave behind it an everlasting fame of a true soldier, who hath done his duty as he was bound to do. But the others of my company have done as traitors and dogs, for which they shall be reproached all their lives and leave a shameful name for ever."

These last words were long forgotten or suppressed ; but Dr. Hannay has shown that they form the ending to this otherwise glorious speech. Grenville's fierce and proud nature could not forgive the crime of surrendering the " Revenge." He wished to engulf her in one final act of defiance.

As for Howard's desertion of him it is well to suspend judgement. With an inferior force and those ships undermanned, he had got well away before the Spanish squadrons, but he turned and fought them well into the night. Not

till then did he make off ; and probably he expected the
" Revenge " to do the same. It was the natural course
for her to take. If Grenville resolved to fight on, was
there any reason why the rest of the English force should
be sacrificed as well ? It was a very difficult position ;
and, of course, Howard may be condemned for excess of
prudence, as Grenville may be for excess of daring. But,
after all, a commander-in-chief has to think, not of his
own feelings, but of the interests of his sovereign. These
counselled retirement during the night before a greatly
superior force. Grenville consulted his own code of
chivalry, which was quixotic.

There I think we may let the matter rest. The Royal
Navy needs both types of men—the prudent, who know
when it is time to retire to save an inferior squadron, and
the daring, who fight on when the odds are desperately
against them, and prefer death to retreat. The pity of it
is that both types were yoked unequally together at the
Homeric fight off Flores.

Such incidents as those of Sir Richard Grenville's fight
to the death in the " Revenge " are worth a century of
ordinary service at sea ; for they inspire both sides with
feelings of respect and admiration, and these feelings
banish those of greed and cruelty. The end of the long
struggle with Spain sees the dawn of a better age of
maritime warfare.

Probably it was the Dutch wars which contributed most
potently to the advance of chivalrous customs, as might
be expected with peoples who were nearly akin and of the
same religion. Apart from trade rivalry and the English
demand that the cross of St. George must be saluted at
sea, there was not much to embroil the two peoples. Then
again the Dutch admirals, de Ruyter and van Tromp, were
men of glorious courage—witness the conduct of de Ruyter
in the fight of September 1652, in the chops of the Channel.
With a slightly inferior fleet, and encumbered by merchantmen, he charged twice into Ayscue's mass, and with his
own ship pushed through. Some other Dutchmen could

not win through in the *mêlée* and the result was indecisive in his favour.  But the affair was a moral victory for the Dutch, and largely because de Ruyter had inspired them with his own courage and burning patriotism.

The conduct of a Frisian captain, Douwe Aukes, was typical.  He was captain of an East Indiaman, the " Struisvogel " (Ostrich).  His crew were beset with fear at the superiority of the English about them, and tried to force him to surrender.  Thereupon he retired to the powder magazine, linstock in hand, ready to blow up the ship, and then faced about.  " Take courage, my children, take courage," he cried, " I will show you the way, and, as we cannot withstand our enemies, I will free you from imprisonment."  He then swore to blow up the ship if they talked of surrender.  Thereupon they desisted, and fought on.  De Ruyter asserts that they sank two English ships with 800 men on board.[1]  However this may be, certainly the Dutch covered themselves with glory, and showed themselves the toughest enemies we had ever met at sea.

They won the regard of Blake, and that high-souled warrior evinced it in a characteristic way.  He spared the Dutch fishing fleet in the North Sea—an act of unusual clemency.  I may note here that it was outdone by Cochrane.  In 1806, as captain of the " Pallas," he captured several French fishing-boats off the Île d'Yeu, and, to the intense surprise of the fishermen, bought their fish and let the crews sail away.

It is pleasing to recall these chivalrous traits of our forefathers, especially after a war in which the Germans treated our fisher-folk with revolting cruelty, torpedoing them at sight as if they were combatants.  As is well known, the conduct of the Germans at sea was a relapse into barbarism ; and mankind finds it hard to forgive and forget deeds which recalled the worst traits of maritime warfare in the Ancient World and during the Middle Ages.

[1] Gardiner, " First Dutch War " (N.R.S.), vol. ii. p. 149.

The Dutch Wars are also remarkable for the importance of the opinion of the crews. The voice of the fo'c'sle now begins to count for much, and its tendency is towards fair-play and clemency. Our sailors, on the whole, liked the Dutch sailors. Some of our men refused to serve against them, and so play the game of Louis XIV., in those disgraceful wars in which Charles II. involved us. All along our people had the hidden feeling that the Dutch were our natural allies ; and, that being the case, it is surprising that our fleets fought as well as they did. Splendid bravery was shown by Monk and the best of our officers. Among them stands high the figure of Sir Christopher Mengs. He fell mortally wounded on the last day of that memorable Four Days' Battle fought off the Downs in June 1666. His men so loved him that a dozen of them obtained leave to carry him to his grave. Pepys has described how afterwards they came to the side of his coach, and, with tears in their eyes, begged him and Sir William Coventry to induce the Duke of York (Lord High Admiral) to give them a fire-ship, so that they might drive it into the Dutch array and thus avenge their fallen captain. Mr. Pepys shed tears, but apparently he did nothing ; for that was the time of rottenness in high places, even when the pedestal still was sound.

By the end of the Third Dutch War hostilities at sea had lost their former ferocity, largely because the two peoples were so closely akin in race, religion, and political ideals that even in the midst of the *mêlée* they came to respect and admire one another ; and out of respect and admiration grew an unwritten code of generous conduct, which was impossible in the days of the Spanish monopolist ascendancy. In this connection a word must be said in praise of Grotius and other Dutch writers, who did much to raise the standard of duty in regard to the laws of war. Even now the world hardly realizes how much it owes to that brave and gifted little nation, not only for its conduct of maritime wars, but also for pointing to higher ideals conducive to the preservation of peace.

I feel that I have now embarked on a boundless theme. Time would fail if I sought to tell of the hundredth part of the chivalrous deeds of later days at sea. The life story of Francesco Morosini, the Venetian admiral; of that gallant Frenchman, Suffren; the tremendous duel of the "Vengeur" and "Brunswick" on the glorious First of June; the desperate defence made by Captain Du Petit Thouars of the "Tonnant," who, when mortally wounded at the Nile, is said to have ordered himself to be placed in a barrel of bran to stanch the wound, so that he might encourage his men to hold out to the end in that hopeless fight—all this might engage our attention for an hour. Above all, there is the figure of the chivalrous Nelson. He and his band of brothers showed that it was possible to raise the standard of valour to unimagined heights, and yet to temper valour with mercy. Nothing in his career more annoyed him than the charge that his sending a flag of truce ashore to the Danes at Copenhagen, when victory was inclining to our side, was a device to cheat the enemy of success. The charge will not bear close examination. He sent a flag of truce ashore in order to preclude the necessity of firing on the Danish hulks which had surrendered, but which some of the enemy vessels were uselessly trying to recapture. The day was actually won, and Nelson desired to stop useless slaughter, especially of a people with whom he had keen sympathy. His last prayer, penned before Trafalgar, contained this utterance, "May humanity after victory be the predominant feature in the British fleet."

This quality it was in Nelson which endeared him to his enemies. Thus, Admiral Gravina added his tribute to our greatest seaman. Gravina had commanded the Spanish fleet at Trafalgar. He died not long after, and, as he lay dying, he uttered these words—"I go to join the brave Nelson, the greatest hero of all time."

Doubtless this essay is open to the criticism that it leaves off where it begins to be most interesting. But my aim has been to trace the customs and practice of chivalry at sea back to their dim and doubtful beginnings ; to show how, out of the welter of cruelty and faithlessness which marked the maritime dealings of the early peoples, aye, and down to the sixteenth and seventeenth centuries, there has slowly emerged a higher conception of the oceans, not as a vast covert of lawlessness and cruelty, but rather as an arena for generous competition and stimulating adventure, in which the strong help the weak against the arch-enemy—the sea itself. This higher conception is now the almost universal conception ; and the horror which ran through the world at its infraction by our late enemies is a measure of the distance which mankind has travelled since the ages when *spurlos versenken* was the usual rule of warfare.

I commend this contrast to the notice of dreary croakers who claim that the human race has not advanced in clemency and humanity. It *has* advanced. Only three centuries ago men were constantly murdering each other on the high seas, and little was thought of it. They went afloat at their own risk, and the only defence was to be stronger than the ship, or ships, which you met. To-day what a contrast there is. Piracy has been put down, mainly by the untiring exertions of the British and American navies ; and the remote waters of Melanesia are safer than the English Channel was in the reigns of the early Stuarts. Wrecking has also gone. In place of the wrecker there stands the lifeboatman, whose efforts are worthy to rank with those of the Knights of the Round Table. Finally, when a ship far out at sea is in distress, invisible messages of mercy thrill forth and bring on the scene dozens of would-be rescuers. All this is a development of the last few generations ; and surely it marks an immense advance in human relations. The sea, formerly the haunt of un-bridled ferocity and faithlessness, is now the arena in which the peoples draw nearer together in fruitful intercourse, and, in time of storm, help one another to the utmost, quite irrespective of nationality. Thus chivalry, which was unknown at sea in former ages, and came into vogue little more than three centuries ago, and then only among a few high-minded captains, is now the unwritten code inspiring the actions of every man deserving the name of sailor.

# INDEX

Aboukir Bay, 78, 104, 128-9
  Battle of, 78-9, 93, 104-5, 125, 133, 145, 150, 194
Abydos, 166, 169, 174
Aché, d', Commodore, 84, 85, 88-9, 90-1
Acheen, 92
Achilles, 182
Acre, 106, 123
Addington, Ministry of, 96, 109, 110, 130, 153, 155
Admiralty, British, 5, 7, 14 *et seq.*, 61, 63-4, 76 *et seq.*, 78, 104, 110, 111, 117-19, 140, 160
  German, caution of, 7, 10, 11 *n.*
Aeschylus, 182, 183
Afghanistan, 81
Agadir crisis (1911), 25
Ahmad Shah, 81
Aircraft, 4, 5, 7, 8, 15, 27, 33, 45, 47, 48, 67
  against submarines, 12, 22, 23
Aisne River, 29, 35
Aix-la-Chapelle, Peace of (1748), 73
Alberoni, Cardinal, 72, 80
Albert, 44, 46
Aleppo, 45
Alexander I., Czar, 153, 158, 161, 162
Alexandretta, 94, 129
Alexandria, 104-106, 108, 110, 161
Allenby, General, 44, 45 and *n.*
Alps, 43, 71
Ambleteuse, 111
America, *see* United States
  North, 75, 84, 91
Amiens, 44
  Treaty of (1802), 79, 96, 153-4
Anson, Lord, Admiral, 57, 60, 82, 111, 120
Anti-submarine inventions, 22, 23
Antigua, 117, 134
Antwerp, 35, 65, 109
Arabs and India, 81
Aracan, coast of, 85
Arbuthnot, Rt. Hon. Chas. (Ambassador), 158-176, 163-166
Arcot, 89
Argonauts, 186
Armada, The Spanish, 51 *et seq.*, 98, 112, 183, 185, 187

Armaments, race, 32 ; produce war, 32
Armour, of ships, 3, 4, 25, 26
Arms of troops, 49
Army, national, 6, 29, 31, 32, 33, 43
Artillery (*see also* Gun), 30, 31, 34, 38, 39, 40, 45, 47-49, 100, 106, 109
Aryan, inroads into India, 81
Asia, Central, tribes of, 81
Asia Minor, 178
Asiago plateau, 43
Augereau, General, 109
Austen, T. W., Captain, 135
Austerlitz, Battle of, 43, 118, 125
Austria, 6 *n*, 46, 56, 73, 76-78, 93, 101, 103, 107, 108, 118, 121-2, 127-129, 152
Ayscue, Admiral, 191
Azopardi, Baron, 144, 154 *n*
Azores, 116, 189

Baghdad, 94
Balkan crisis (1908-9), 25
Ball, Sir Alexander, Captain, R.N., 142, 146-7, 149, 150-1, 154
Baltic Sea, 20 *n*, 110, 130-1, 153, 176
Baluchistan, tribes of, 81
Bantry Bay, 63, 64
Bapaume, 40, 41, 43, 44
Barbados, 132
Barbary pirates, 80
Barcelona, 71
Barfleur, Battle of, 13
Barham, Lord, 118, 121
Barrage, creeping, 40
Bartolo, Dr. Augusto, 144
Base, naval, *see* Scapa Flow, Wilhelmshafen, Malta, etc.
Basra, 129
Bastia, 126
Batavian Republic, 62
Bathurst, Earl, 143
Baticaloa, 92, 95
Battleships, Japanese, 3
  Russian, 3
  a compromise, 26
Bayntum, H. W., Captain, R.N., 135
Bayonne, 123
Beachy Head, Battle of, 2, 27, 56
Beatty, Vice-Admiral, 13 *et seq.*

197